THE MIRROR PROBLEM

HOW AI REFLECTS OUR WORST SELVES

THE ALGORITHMIC MIND
BOOK 1

GARI JOHNSON

GTM APAC

The Mirror Problem: How AI Reflects Our Worst Selves

Book 1: The Algorithmic Mind Series

Published by Gari Johnson Books, Sydney, Australia.

Second edition, 2026. First published 2025.

Series Information:

The Algorithmic Mind is a three-book series that examines the impact of artificial intelligence on society and human agency.

- Book 1: The Mirror Problem, How AI Reflects Our Worst Selves
- Book 2: The Surveillance Mirror, How AI Shapes Human Behaviour
- Book 3: The Human Interface, Adapting to Life with AI

Cover and interior design by the Author

Disclaimer:

The views and opinions expressed in this book are those of the author and do not necessarily reflect the official policy or position of any organisation, employer, or institution with which the author has been affiliated. The information provided is for educational and informational purposes only.

This book contains both real examples and composite illustrations. Composite voices are drawn from documented patterns rather than specific individuals; they are identifiable by the absence of footnote cues – any voice without a superscript note is a composite. Where real research, companies, or events are referenced, proper citations are provided.

Contact Information: For speaking engagements, media enquiries, or bulk sales, please contact the author. Email: gari.johnson@icloud.com Website: www.gtmapac.com

Publisher's Note: This book contains references to real companies, products, and services for illustrative purposes. All trademarks and trade names are the property of their respective owners and are used here for identification purposes only.

Formatted with Vellum

FOREWORD: THE MACHINE IN THE MIRROR

OR HOW I LEARNED TO STOP WORRYING AND LOVE THE ALGORITHM

A panel of predominantly white, male engineers from leading AI companies sat on a San Francisco stage and discussed the 'democratising power of artificial intelligence.' The irony was thick enough to mine for bitcoin. Here were representatives of the most homogeneous industry in modern history, creating systems they claimed would eliminate bias, speaking to an audience of investors whose diversity statistics would make a 1950s country club look like a UNESCO meeting.

'Our algorithms don't see race,' declared one panellist, apparently unaware that his company's facial recognition system had recently mistaken three Black members of Congress for criminals. The audience nodded approvingly, perhaps missing the deeper irony that creating systems that 'don't see race' in a world shaped by racial injustice might be less progressive than it sounds.

This book explores the central paradox of contemporary artificial intelligence: we have created systems designed to eliminate human bias, yet built on the most biased development process in technological history. We have built machines intended to be objective arbiters of truth while feeding them data that reflects centuries of discrimination. We have designed algorithms to serve all humanity while concentrating their development in a handful of companies staffed by people who look remarkably similar to one another.

THE MIRROR AND THE MYTH

The title *The Mirror Problem* deliberately invokes both the literal algorithmic challenges we face and the metaphorical reflection of human society that AI systems provide. When recruitment algorithms discriminate against women, when facial recognition fails for anyone who is not white, when predictive policing perpetuates racial profiling, these systems are not malfunctioning. They are working exactly as designed, reflecting the patterns in their training data with ruthless efficiency.

Mirrors can serve different purposes. They can reveal truths we would rather not see, forcing us to confront uncomfortable realities. Or they can become tools of narcissism, reflecting only what we want to see while distorting everything else. The question is not whether AI reflects human society. It inevitably does. The question is whether we will use that reflection for recognition and improvement, or allow it to justify and perpetuate existing inequalities.

A NOTE ON SOURCES AND VOICES

This book contains both real, documented material and composite illustrative examples. The real cases are cited with numbered notes. Amazon's recruiting algorithm that downgraded women's CVs – that happened.[1] Google's photo recognition labelling Black people as gorillas – that happened.[2] Predictive policing systems that targeted neighbourhoods based on racist historical data – happening right now in cities across the world.

The composite examples illustrate patterns without the legal or privacy complications of naming real people. You can tell them apart by one mark. Composite voices carry *no* note cue. A character who speaks but carries no superscript number is a composite, assembled from patterns documented across dozens of real cases. A character whose words are followed by a number is drawing on sourced material.

This convention (no cue for composite voices, numbered cues for documented claims) applies throughout the book. It is stated here once, clearly, so that readers can tell the two apart without interruption.

A NOTE ON COLLABORATION

This book was written with extensive assistance from Claude, an AI system developed by Anthropic, and edited with Grammarly. The collaboration revealed both the potential and limitations of human-AI partnerships. Claude helped identify research, suggested structural approaches, and occasionally generated passages that captured ideas more crisply than my initial attempts. But Claude also exhibited biases, made errors, and sometimes produced eloquent nonsense that sounded profound until you thought about it for ten seconds.

I disclose this because pretending the book sprang from human creativity alone would be dishonest, and claiming an AI produced it would be equally false. The truth sits between the two, and it is messier than either version. Every passage Claude suggested was checked, argued with, and frequently rewritten. The machine was a collaborator, not an author, and a collaborator who needed watching.

A NOTE ON CURRENCY AND THE READER

This is the second edition, reflecting the state of play as of mid-2026. Where the first edition's claims have been corrected, the corrections follow the best evidence I could find, and the few figures that cannot be independently checked are kept as printed and flagged in the notes. No specialist background is needed to read what follows. If an algorithm has ever made a decision about your money, your job, or your face, this book is written for you.

PART I

THE DIVERSITY PARADOX

1

THE EMPEROR'S NEW ALGORITHM

The annual diversity report arrived with predictable fanfare. A major Silicon Valley AI company celebrated reaching 23% female technical staff, up from 21%. Buried in the appendices: their new performance evaluation algorithm had been rating men higher than women for identical work.[3]

The system had been trained on five years of historical data, learning that maleness correlated with high ratings, not through superior performance, but through embedded managerial bias. The machine had not developed sexism; it had perfected it, transforming subjective prejudice into mathematics that seemed objective.

This exemplifies the emperor's new algorithm: systems promising objectivity while systematising subjectivity, claiming to eliminate bias even as they emerge from the most homogeneous workforce in modern industry. The technology sector has convinced itself, and much of the world, that mathematical models transcend human prejudice. The reality proves considerably messier and significantly less flattering.

THE STATISTICAL MIRAGE OF OBJECTIVITY

Machine learning does not eliminate human judgment. It automates it at an unprecedented scale. Every dataset embeds decisions about what matters. Every optimisation function encodes values. Every metric reflects assumptions about success. The myth of algorithmic objectivity rests on a fundamental misunderstanding of how these systems actually function.

Consider microfinance AI in Kenya. European-developed systems consistently denied loans to pastoralist communities whose irregular income patterns, tied to rainfall and livestock cycles, appeared risky to algorithms trained on steady wage assumptions.[4] The technology could not distinguish economic instability from a different, yet sustainable, economic model that had supported communities for millennia.

The algorithm had learned from European data that regular income indicates creditworthiness, a reasonable assumption in contexts where employment means fixed salaries. But Kenyan pastoralists measure wealth in cattle, whose value fluctuates with seasons but represents genuine economic security. The AI system interpreted this variability as instability, denying credit to some of the most economically resilient communities in East Africa.

When South African banks deployed similar systems, they discovered the algorithms penalised township addresses, effectively redlining via mathematics.[5] The systems were not malfunctioning; they were faithfully reproducing historical lending discrimination at digital speed. Applicants from Soweto faced systematic rejection, regardless of their individual creditworthiness, as the algorithm had learned that certain postcodes correlated with loan defaults, a correlation created by decades of economic exclusion. Inherent risk had nothing to do with it.

The South African experience revealed another layer of algorithmic bias: language prejudice. Applications written in English received higher scores than those in Afrikaans or indigenous languages, even when the content was identical. The natural language processing system had learned from training data that 'professional' communication meant English, specifically the kind used by university-educated loan officers. Township applicants who spoke English as a third or fourth language were algorithmically deemed less creditworthy based on linguistic markers that had nothing to do with their ability to repay loans.

Healthcare AI demonstrates similar patterns of encoded prejudice. An algorithm used across NHS trusts to allocate community nursing resources to underserved South Asian populations in a consistent pattern.[6] The system had learned that these communities historically received fewer home visits, interpreting access barriers as lower need. Families who could not find their way through the healthcare system due to language barriers or cultural unfamiliarity were algorithmically recorded as not requiring services they desperately needed.

The NHS case exposed how algorithms transform structural inequalities into seemingly objective resource allocation. South Asian families often provided intergenerational care at home, reducing their historical use of community nursing services. The AI interpreted this as lower need. It was a different care model, not evidence of lower need. When these families did need professional nursing support, often in crisis situations, the algorithm had already classified their neighbourhoods as low-priority.

THE MECHANICS OF DISCRIMINATION

Modern AI discrimination operates through sophisticated pattern recognition that identifies and amplifies historical bias. These systems achieve what humans never could: consistent, scaled, mathematically justified prejudice.

Recruitment provides clear examples beyond the well-documented cases at major tech companies. A retail chain's scheduling algorithm in Japan consistently assigned women to lower-paid morning shifts, having learned that female employees historically worked these hours due to childcare responsibilities.[7] The system perpetuated gendered labour divisions while claiming optimal efficiency. When questioned, the algorithm's developers insisted it was 'gender-blind' because it did not explicitly consider gender, only historical scheduling patterns that happened to correlate perfectly with gender.

Educational AI amplifies academic segregation through feedback mechanisms that transform temporary disadvantage into permanent exclusion. Adaptive learning platforms in Brazil recommended vocational tracks to students from favelas while suggesting academic paths for middle-class students with identical performance.[8] The algorithm had learned that postal codes predicted educational outcomes, then helped ensure they continued to do so.

The Brazilian education system's AI went further, adjusting difficulty levels based on socioeconomic indicators. Students from poorer neighbourhoods received 'scaffolded' content that moved more slowly, based on the assumption they needed more support. This meant favela students literally received a different education than their wealthy peers, creating achievement gaps that justified the original differentiation. The algorithm made the educational inequality it purported to address.

GEOGRAPHIC AND INFRASTRUCTURE BIAS

AI systems consistently privilege urban areas over rural ones, wealthy individuals over those who are poor, and connected individuals over those who are disconnected. This is not intentional. It is structural, embedded in the data these systems consume and the assumptions they encode about what constitutes 'normal' living conditions.

Agricultural AI developed for industrial farming proves catastrophic when deployed to smallholder contexts. In Maharashtra, India, a precision agriculture system recommended fertiliser applications that would cost more than farmers' annual income.[9] The algorithm optimised yields without understanding economic constraints, having been trained on data from farms where input costs were negligible compared to revenue.

The Maharashtra case exposed multiple layers of geographic bias. The AI system assumed farmers had access to credit, could afford crop insurance, and could weather a bad season. It recommended monoculture planting for efficiency, ignoring that crop diversity was these farmers' only insurance against total loss. The algorithm's 'precision' was precisely wrong for the context in which it was deployed.

Voice recognition systems trained on urban speech patterns fail dramatically in rural contexts. Welsh farmers report agricultural monitoring systems that cannot understand their accents.[10] The technology works perfectly in London but fails completely in Llanfairpwllgwyngyll. This is not just an inconvenience: when voice-controlled safety systems fail to interpret warnings, linguistic bias can be life-threatening.

The Welsh example highlights how AI systems encode assumptions about 'standard' language that marginalise linguistic diversity. The voice recognition system had been trained on Received Pronunciation and London-accented English, treating Welsh-accented English as a deviation from a norm it should not have set. Farmers had to adopt fake English accents to interact with systems meant to serve them.

Telemedicine AI exhibits similar urban bias. Systems trained on high-resolution medical imaging from well-equipped hospitals struggle with the lower-quality images available in rural clinics.[11] A melanoma detection algorithm that achieved 95% accuracy at Stanford dropped to 60% accuracy when applied to images from mobile clinics in Guatemala.[12] The AI's sophistication became useless when deployed outside the privileged contexts for which it was designed.

Infrastructure assumptions pervade AI systems in ways their creators rarely recognise. Educational AI assumes a reliable internet connection; financial AI assumes bank accounts (which approximately 1.4 billion adults lack[13]); and healthcare AI assumes medical records that are non-existent for billions. These systems do not just fail marginalised populations. They were not designed with these populations' existence in mind.

THE ECONOMIC INCENTIVES BEHIND BIAS

Understanding why AI systems consistently discriminate requires examining the economic structures that incentivise bias. These are not accidents but predictable outcomes of how AI development is funded, how success is measured, and who profits from deployment.

Venture capital funding for AI flows overwhelmingly to companies serving affluent markets. Critics have argued that much AI investment is oriented towards markets serving affluent consumers, with comparatively little focus on the challenges facing the majority of the world's population, a point documented extensively by AI researchers examining research agendas skewed towards wealthy-world problems.[14] This creates an AI optimised for problems wealthy people have while ignoring challenges faced by the global majority. The bias is not in the code. It is in the capitalism that funds the coding.

Corporate AI development prioritises efficiency metrics that encode bias. When Amazon's recruitment algorithm downgraded women's applications, it was optimising for the metric it was given: matching historical hiring patterns.[15] The company measured success by how closely AI recommendations aligned with human decisions, ensuring the algorithm would reproduce human biases. The economic incentive was to hire quickly and cheaply, not fairly.

The efficiency bias appears throughout commercial AI. Customer service chatbots optimised for call resolution speed learn to end conversations with marginalised customers who need more support. Loan approval systems optimised for default minimisation learn to exclude entire communities; individual creditworthiness ceases to be the question. Healthcare AI optimised for cost reduction learns to under-treat populations whose health problems are expensive to solve.

Platform economics creates additional biased incentives. Social media algorithms optimise for engagement, which research shows comes from content that confirms existing beliefs and triggers strong emotions.[16] This economically incentivises AI systems to create echo chambers, amplify extremism, and polarise communities. The platforms profit from division while claiming to connect people.

The engagement economy's bias extends beyond political polarisation. Instagram's algorithm learns to promote content that makes users feel inadequate. YouTube learns to recommend increasingly extreme content. TikTok learns to surface content that triggers addictive behaviours. These biases serve shareholder value while damaging user well-being.

THE AUDIT GAP

Understanding the mirror problem requires understanding something counterintuitive about how AI systems are built and deployed: the organisations most affected by algorithmic decisions are typically the last to learn how those systems work.

A benefits agency deploys a fraud detection algorithm. The algorithm flags claimants for investigation. The claimants' lives are materially affected. The fraud detection vendor considers the algorithm proprietary. The agency's procurement staff lack the technical capacity to evaluate the vendor's claims. Auditors examining the agency's accounts have no mandate to assess algorithmic performance. No independent body routinely tests whether the system's error rates are evenly distributed across demographic groups.

This is not a hypothetical. It is the documented governance environment in which most public-sector algorithmic systems currently operate. The people bearing the costs of algorithmic errors have the least access to information about why they occur.

The audit gap has three components. The first is technical: many AI systems are genuinely difficult to audit because they are complex, their outputs are probabilistic, and their decision processes cannot be reduced to a simple rule set that auditors can check. The second is legal: intellectual property protections, commercial confidentiality agreements, and the absence of mandatory disclosure requirements combine to shield systems from external scrutiny. The third is institutional: the organisations responsible for oversight typically lack the technical expertise to conduct meaningful audits even when access is granted.

Closing the audit gap requires addressing all three components simultaneously. Research on technical interpretability is making progress on the first. Regulatory change is the only path to the second. Building institutional technical capacity is the hardest and slowest, and it is the one receiving the least attention.

The individuals and communities bearing the costs of inadequate auditing are not waiting patiently for the governance gap to close. Legal challenges, investigative journalism, civil society audits, and community organising are all producing information about how these systems perform in practice. The pattern of findings is consistent enough to establish that the gap is not an isolated oversight. It is a structural feature of how AI has been deployed in the absence of adequate governance.

WHAT THE FIRST EDITION GOT WRONG

This second edition corrects factual errors present in the first. Most were errors of attribution: findings assigned to the wrong study, statistics from real research misquoted or miscontextualised. They are corrected throughout this text and documented in the editorial register.

Some were errors of framing. The first edition described the problem of AI bias in terms that suggested it was primarily a technical problem amenable to technical solutions: better training data, more diverse teams, improved algorithms. This framing was not wrong, but it was incomplete. The evidence accumulated since the first edition was written suggests that the deeper sources of algorithmic harm are structural. Inadequate governance, insufficient accountability, regulatory frameworks designed for an earlier era, and the concentration of AI development in institutions whose interests do not align with the interests of the people most affected by the systems they build: these are not technical problems.

Technical fixes that leave these structural conditions intact will not resolve the mirror problem. Better facial recognition will still be deployed in contexts where its use violates rights. Debiased credit models will still be used by lenders who lack adequate accountability to affected borrowers. More accurate recidivism predictions will still feed into sentencing frameworks that produce racially disparate outcomes. The bias in the mirror is real and worth reducing. The frame around the mirror is the larger problem.

2

WHEN MACHINES LEARN TO DISCRIMINATE

The concept of machine learning discrimination seems paradoxical. Machines lack consciousness, prejudice, or social conditioning. They have no ideology, no upbringing, no cultural baggage. Yet they discriminate with remarkable efficiency, having learned to recognise and reproduce human bias patterns with mathematical precision that surpasses human prejudice in both scale and consistency.

Understanding how machines learn to discriminate requires examining the technical processes through which bias becomes embedded in algorithmic decision-making. This is not a story of malicious programming but of systems faithfully learning from biased data, optimising for biased objectives, and being evaluated by biased metrics.

THE ANATOMY OF ALGORITHMIC PREJUDICE

Machine learning systems learn discrimination through pattern recognition in training data. They identify statistical correlations (postcode with loan default, name with job performance, speech pattern with criminality) and transform these into predictive rules.

The process appears objective because it is mathematical, but applying mathematics to biased data yields biased results with mathematical certainty.

Facial recognition offers the starkest example. The Gender Shades study, conducted at the MIT Media Lab, found that commercial facial-recognition classifiers misclassified dark-skinned women 34.7% of the time, compared with an error rate of just 0.8% for light-skinned men.[17] The disparity was not a programming failure but training data that treated whiteness as the default, and everything else as deviation. The system had learned to see light-skinned faces with nuance while viewing dark-skinned faces as variations on a theme. This finding was subsequently reinforced by the Face Recognition Vendor Test from NIST, the US National Institute of Standards and Technology, which found that African American females had the highest false-positive rates of any demographic group tested.[18]

This technical discrimination extends to the mathematical operations underlying facial recognition. The eigenfaces approach, built on Principal Component Analysis, naturally emphasises variations that appear most frequently in training data. When the data predominantly features lighter-skinned faces, the algorithm develops sophisticated discrimination capabilities for those features while remaining crude in recognising others. The maths is not racist, but maths applied to racist data produces racist outcomes.

Similar patterns emerge in emotion detection. Systems trained primarily on European faces consistently misread expressions from East Asian users as 'neutral' or 'unhappy' due to differing cultural norms of expression.[19] A smile that registers as 'genuine' for Western faces might be perceived as 'forced' for Asian faces, not through malice, but through monocultural training that treats Western expressions as universal.

The emotion detection bias reveals how algorithms encode cultural assumptions about internal states. Western training data associates broad smiles with happiness, direct eye contact with honesty, and animated expressions with engagement. East Asian cultures that value emotional restraint, indirect gaze as respect, and subtle expression get algorithmically classified as unhappy, deceptive, or disengaged.

Language processing reveals subtler discrimination. Natural language AI trained on professional communication consistently rates writing from non-native English speakers as 'less intelligent' or 'less competent'.[20] The systems have learned to associate linguistic features of standard American English with authority and expertise, interpreting variation as deficiency. Research on AI writing-detection tools has found that these systems disproportionately flag non-native English speakers as potential AI writers, penalising natural variation in syntax. The systems flag the wrong thing.[21]

FEEDBACK LOOPS AND AMPLIFICATION

Algorithmic discrimination becomes self-reinforcing through feedback mechanisms that make bias appear justified by its own consequences. These feedback loops operate at multiple scales (immediate, medium-term, and generational) creating cascading discrimination that becomes increasingly difficult to interrupt.

In the Netherlands, a government fraud detection algorithm flagged approximately 26,000 families for benefits investigation, devastating lives through false accusations.[22] The system had learned that dual nationality correlated with fraud, primarily because previous investigations had disproportionately targeted immigrant communities. Each investigation, regardless of outcome, reinforced the pattern, creating a statistical correlation that justified continued discrimination.

The Dutch case, known as the *toeslagenaffaire* (benefits affair), destroyed families. Parents lost jobs due to fraud investigations, children were removed from homes when families could not afford care, and marriages collapsed under financial pressure. The algorithm's false accusations created real crises, making the affected families more likely to exhibit the 'risk factors' the system monitored. Discrimination became self-validating through the devastation it caused.

Criminal justice provides another feedback mechanism. New

Zealand's risk-assessment tools have been shown to assign Māori defendants higher predicted recidivism scores, even after controlling for prior criminal history: a disparity that researchers attribute in part to biased upstream policing and prosecution data encoded into the algorithm's training set.[23] Higher risk scores led to harsher sentences, which increased actual reoffending through disrupted employment and family relationships, appearing to validate the original assessment.

The New Zealand system exposed generational feedback loops. Children whose parents received harsh sentences based on algorithmic risk scores were more likely to enter the justice system themselves. The algorithm learned this pattern and began assigning higher risk scores to defendants whose parents had criminal records. Discrimination literally became hereditary, passed down through datasets that treated family history as predictive, with no mechanism to account for how the system itself had created that history.

Financial systems demonstrate long-term feedback effects. When algorithmic credit scoring in the Philippines began incorporating social media data, it created cascading discrimination.[24] Individuals in lower-income networks had worse credit scores, which limited their economic opportunities and reinforced the economic segregation that the algorithm identified. Social connections became proxies for creditworthiness, creating pressure to distance oneself from struggling community members and fragmenting mutual aid systems that helped communities survive poverty.

THE TRAINING DATA PROBLEM

The foundation of machine-learning discrimination lies in training data that embed historical patterns of human prejudice. These datasets, often celebrated for their size and comprehensiveness, contain within them the sedimentary layers of centuries of discrimination, which algorithms learn to recognise and reproduce.

Medical training data exemplifies this problem. The overwhelming majority of medical research has historically focused on white male subjects.[25] When AI systems train on this data, they learn that white male physiology is 'normal' and everything else is deviation. Heart attack symptoms in women, drug metabolism in African populations, disease presentation in Asian patients, all become edge cases that the algorithm struggles to recognise.

A study published in *Science* found that a widely used health-care risk-prediction algorithm, applied to tens of millions of Americans, assigned Black patients the same risk level as white patients even when the Black patients were considerably sicker. Correcting the bias would have increased the proportion of Black patients referred for additional care from 17.7% to 46.5%.[26] The system had learned from training data where Black patients were underrepresented, misdiagnosed, and underserved. It reproduced these patterns with perfect fidelity.

Employment training data carries decades of workplace discrimination. When LinkedIn developed recruitment AI, it trained on successful employee profiles from major corporations.[27] These profiles reflected generations of hiring bias: predominantly male, overwhelmingly white, disproportionately from elite universities. The AI learned that success looked like historical privilege, screening out anyone who did not match patterns created by discrimination.

The employment data revealed how bias compounds through proxy variables. The algorithm learned that certain universities predicted success (because discriminatory hiring had created alumni networks), certain activities indicated leadership (because men had historically had access to them), and certain postcodes suggested reliability (because residential segregation concentrated privilege). Each proxy variable appeared statistically valid while actually measuring the effects of historical discrimination.

CULTURAL AND LINGUISTIC TRAINING BIAS

Training data does not just embed demographic bias. It encodes entire worldviews, cultural assumptions, and linguistic hierarchies that AI systems learn to treat as universal truth.

Chinese AI researchers discovered that emotion recognition systems trained on Western data consistently misclassified Chinese expressions.[28] The systems had learned that emotional expression follows Western patterns: direct, individual, explicit. Chinese emotional expression, which emphasises collective harmony, contextual appropriateness, and subtle indications, was classified as 'emotionally flat' or 'deceptive' by Western-trained algorithms.

Arabic language processing faces unique challenges from training data bias. Most Arabic NLP systems train on Modern Standard Arabic (MSA), the formal written language used in media and literature.[29] But most Arabic speakers communicate in regional dialects that differ dramatically from MSA. AI systems trained on MSA literally cannot understand how most Arabic speakers actually communicate, creating linguistic discrimination that excludes millions from AI services.

The Arabic case exposes how training data choices embed political and social hierarchies. MSA is associated with education, formality, and authority. Dialectical Arabic is associated with informality and lower social status. By training exclusively on MSA, AI systems reproduce linguistic hierarchies that marginalise speakers of 'lesser' variants, transforming linguistic diversity into algorithmic exclusion.

Indigenous languages face existential threats from training data bias. With limited written corpora and few digital resources, indigenous languages are essentially invisible to AI systems.[30] A study of AI translation for Native American languages found error rates exceeding 70%, with systems consistently imposing English grammatical structures on languages with fundamentally different organisational principles.[31] The AI had not learned to translate. It had learned to force indigenous expression into English conceptual frameworks.

BIAS AMPLIFICATION: THE FEEDBACK ARCHITECTURE

Algorithmic bias does not merely reflect existing discrimination. It amplifies and entrenches it through feedback mechanisms that make prejudice appear natural and justified. These loops operate at multiple scales: immediate, institutional, and generational.

Immediate feedback occurs when algorithmic decisions directly create the outcomes they predict. A hiring algorithm that disproportionately rejects women for technical roles leads to male-dominated teams. These teams develop products that work better for men, succeed in male-dominated markets, and serve as examples of 'successful' teams that train future algorithms. The initial discrimination becomes 'proof' that the discrimination was justified.

A software company discovered this loop in devastating detail.[32] Their AI hiring system had learned that successful engineers came from specific universities, participated in competitive programming contests, and contributed to open-source projects, all activities with significant gender disparities. When they hired based on these criteria, they created teams that replicated these patterns, whose success reinforced the original criteria. Male-dominated teams created workplace cultures hostile to women: long hours that ignored caregiving responsibilities, aggressive communication styles, and social events centred on male interests. Women who were hired despite the algorithm's bias often left, which the system interpreted as evidence that women were indeed a higher risk.

Institutional feedback operates through organisational structures that transform individual bias into systemic discrimination. In education, AI systems that track students into different academic paths create institutional feedback loops.[33] Schools allocate resources based on AI classifications: advanced resources for 'gifted' students, remedial resources for 'struggling' students. These resource allocations create the performance differences the AI predicted.

A particularly damaging example emerged in California schools, where AI was used to assess reading levels.[34] The system classified

English language learners as 'below grade level' based on language patterns. Comprehension was not what was being measured. Schools responded by placing these students in remedial reading programmes that were actually below their cognitive ability.

Generational feedback operates across time, transforming temporary disadvantage into inherited inequality. Predictive policing algorithms direct enforcement to neighbourhoods with a history of arrests.[35] An increased police presence leads to more arrests for behaviours that would otherwise go unnoticed elsewhere. Children growing up in these neighbourhoods often have criminal records for activities that their suburban peers engage in without consequence. When these children become adults, algorithms classify them as high risk based on their records and their neighbourhood, directing even more enforcement toward the next generation.

BREAKING THE CYCLE

Interrupting feedback loops requires recognising that biased outcomes are not natural but manufactured. Technical solutions alone cannot address problems rooted in systemic inequality. Breaking these cycles demands fundamental changes in how AI systems are designed, deployed, and governed.

Some organisations have developed 'counterfactual fairness' approaches, testing what outcomes would occur in alternative scenarios.[36] If a loan application would be approved with only the applicant's name changed, the system flags potential discrimination. This reveals discrimination but does not address the underlying feedback loops that created the discriminatory patterns.

A more direct approach involves explicitly considering protected characteristics to actively counter discrimination.[37] Rather than pretending to be 'blind' to race or gender, these systems actively monitor and correct for discriminatory patterns. If an AI system notices it is rejecting qualified women, it adjusts its decision-making to counter this bias.

Community oversight provides another intervention point. In

Barcelona, neighbourhood groups audit municipal algorithms, identifying feedback loops that technical monitoring misses.[38] Their local knowledge reveals how algorithmic decisions create the problems they purport to solve. Residents noticed that crime prediction algorithms directed police to areas with schools, community centres, and public transport: places where people gathered, not where crime was concentrated. The increased police presence criminalised normal community activity, creating arrest records that justified continued intensive policing.

Temporal interventions, deliberately breaking historical patterns, show promise. Some universities now train admission algorithms on aspirational data representing desired diversity, not historical admission patterns.[39] This reverses feedback loops, using algorithmic power to create change. Merely reflecting existing inequality was the problem.

3

THE WHITENESS OF AI

The AI industry's demographic concentration exceeds even traditional technology sectors. This uniformity does not just limit perspectives. It fundamentally shapes what AI systems see, understand, and value. The 'whiteness' of AI transcends racial composition, encompassing cultural assumptions, epistemological frameworks, and definitions of intelligence itself.

BEYOND DEMOGRAPHICS

While the statistics are stark (the 2018 NVCA-Deloitte Human Capital Survey found that white employees comprised 77% of investment partners at US venture capital firms, with women making up just 11% of investment partners[40]), the deeper issue is how this homogeneity shapes the fundamental assumptions embedded in AI systems deployed globally.

The whiteness of AI manifests in what problems are deemed worth solving. Critics have noted that AI research agendas have historically been oriented towards the problems of wealthy institutions and consumers, with comparatively little focus on the challenges facing the majority of the world's population.[41] Optimising ad targeting, personalising shopping recommendations, and automating luxury services attract massive investment, while the challenges facing the global majority remain largely ignored.

Consider the contrast: Silicon Valley has produced dozens of AI companies focused on optimising food delivery for urban professionals, but almost none addressing food security for the 2 billion people facing malnutrition.[42] There are AI systems that can recommend the perfect wine pairing, but none that can help subsistence farmers optimise crop selection for changing climate conditions. The bias is not just in how AI systems work. It is in which AI systems get built.

African researchers have documented how Western AI misunderstands communal decision-making. In Ghana, a healthcare AI system failed because it assumed individual medical consent, conflicting with family-based healthcare decisions.[43] The system's Western individualism rendered it effectively unusable, not through technical failure, but through cultural incompetence.

When the system recommended cancer treatment that would bankrupt an extended family, it optimised for individual survival probability without understanding that treatment decisions involved weighing one person's health against the educational opportunities of a dozen children, the business capital of siblings, the retirement security of elders. The AI's individual focus disrupted family decision-making processes that had been in place for generations.

Indigenous knowledge systems face particular erasure. Agricultural AI dismisses traditional farming practices as 'inefficient' without understanding their ecological sustainability.[44] In Peru, an AI-driven agricultural programme pushed farmers to abandon traditional crop diversity for monocultures that the algorithm deemed 'optimal', until climate variations destroyed the narrowly chosen crops.

The Peruvian example exposed how AI systems encode assumptions about agricultural 'progress.' The algorithm measured success through yield per hectare, water efficiency, and input optimisation, metrics that made sense for industrial agriculture but missed important dimensions of traditional farming. It could not value crop diversity as a risk management tool, traditional varieties as genetic resources, or farming practices as a form of cultural preservation.

LANGUAGE AS POWER

The dominance of English in AI development creates cascading exclusions. Of the world's 7,000 languages, fewer than 100 have meaningful AI support.[45] This is not mere inconvenience. It is a form of intellectual violence, erasing ways of knowing that do not fit into English computational frameworks.

Consider Sanskrit's compound-word construction, which conveys meanings that would require paragraphs in English. AI translation systems, designed around English grammar, cannot process these semantic structures.[46] Ancient mathematical and philosophical texts become incomprehensible when filtered through English-centric AI, erasing thousands of years of intellectual tradition.

The problem compounds in education. AI tutoring systems designed for English-medium instruction disadvantage students whose first-language structures of knowledge differ.[47] In Malaysia, students who think in Bahasa perform worse on AI-evaluated assessments, not through lack of knowledge but through linguistic mismatch. Malaysian students report having to 'translate their thoughts twice': first from Bahasa conceptual structures to English, then from natural English to the specific English patterns the AI expects.

The linguistic imperialism extends to professional contexts. AI-powered hiring systems trained on English business communication penalise qualified candidates who communicate professionally in other languages.[48] A software engineer who writes elegant code but imperfect English emails gets algorithmically classified as less competent than a native English speaker with mediocre programming skills.

THE VENTURE CAPITAL ECHO CHAMBER

The whiteness of AI is reinforced and amplified by venture capital networks that are even more uniform than the engineering teams they fund.

Research by digitalundivided, a US non-profit focused on Black and Latina women entrepreneurs, through its *ProjectDiane* project, found that Black women-founded companies received approximately 0.27% of all US venture capital investment in 2018-19, in a funding landscape where the vast majority of capital flowed to companies led by white men.[49] This is not just unequal. It is algorithmic in its precision, with funding decisions following patterns as predictable as any machine learning model.

The funding bias creates compound effects. White male founders hire white male engineers who build AI for white male users, creating systems that work brilliantly for people like their creators while failing everyone else. When these companies succeed (by serving their narrow market well), they attract more funding, hire more people like them, and embed their assumptions more deeply into AI infrastructure.

A Black female founder developing healthcare AI for underserved communities described the funding challenge: 'VCs kept asking about our "total addressable market" as if Black women's health was a niche issue. They wanted to know how we'd expand to "mainstream" users, meaning white users. The assumption was that technology for Black women was inherently limited while technology for white men was universal.'

The venture capital echo chamber extends beyond demographics to ideology. Funders share assumptions about what technology should do (disrupt, not support), how it should work (scale, not adapt), and whom it should serve (consumers, not citizens). These assumptions become embedded in every AI system they fund.

EDUCATIONAL PIPELINES AND KNOWLEDGE HIERARCHIES

The whiteness of AI begins in educational institutions that treat Western approaches to knowledge as universal while marginalising other intellectual traditions.

Computer science curricula at major universities overwhelmingly emphasise Western mathematical approaches, Western philosophical frameworks, and Western definitions of intelligence.[50] Alternative methods (Indigenous pattern recognition, African communal problem-solving, Asian contextual reasoning) are absent from the education that produces AI developers.

A Nigerian computer scientist educated at MIT described the cognitive dissonance: 'I had to unlearn my culture's approaches to knowledge to succeed in Western computer science. The programme taught me that real intelligence was individual, explicit, and mathematical. The communal, contextual, and narrative intelligence of my culture was treated as primitive. Now I build AI systems that embed the same hierarchy.'

The knowledge hierarchy extends to research priorities. Academic AI research, driven by publication metrics and grant funding, concentrates on problems that interest Western academics.[51] Papers on optimising Netflix recommendations outnumber papers on optimising smallholder agriculture 100 to 1. The subject is not more technically interesting; it aligns with Western academic priorities.

MEDICAL AI AND RACIAL HEALTH DISPARITIES

Healthcare AI starkly reveals how the whiteness of AI development becomes a matter of life and death. Medical AI systems trained on data from predominantly white populations fail when treating patients of colour.

Pulse oximetry AI, used to monitor oxygen levels in critically ill patients, shows significantly higher rates of undetected dangerous hypoxaemia in Black patients than white patients. A study published in the *New England Journal of Medicine* found that occult hypoxaemia went undetected in 17.0% of Black patients versus 6.2% of white patients: nearly three times the frequency.[52] The devices were calibrated on lighter-skinned individuals, and the AI systems trained on their output learned to interpret readings based on a white physiological baseline. During COVID-19, this meant Black patients were consistently under-treated for respiratory distress because AI systems misread their oxygen levels.

Dermatology AI shows stark disparities. Dermatology AI systems trained predominantly on images of lighter-skinned patients substantially underperform when applied to darker skin tones.[53] The systems were trained on image datasets where the overwhelming majority of examples showed skin conditions on white patients. They had not learned what cancer looks like on dark skin. Melanoma in Black patients is often diagnosed at later stages when survival rates drop sharply. AI systems that miss early-stage cancers in Black patients while over-diagnosing benign conditions in white patients do not just reflect health disparities. They actively worsen them.

Psychiatric AI reveals how cultural assumptions about mental health become embedded in diagnostic systems. AI trained on Western psychiatric frameworks consistently misdiagnoses mental health conditions in non-Western populations.[54] A study in Kenya found that psychiatric AI classified everyday grief expressions in Kikuyu culture as major depression requiring medication.[55] The system had learned Western assumptions about appropriate emotional expression and mourning periods. Meanwhile, it missed actual depression expressed through somatic symptoms that Western psychiatry does not associate with mental illness.

WHEN SILICON VALLEY DEFINES INTELLIGENCE

The homogeneity problem in AI development has a specific intellectual dimension that matters beyond demographics: it determines whose definition of intelligence becomes the default for machine learning systems.

Western cognitive science, the primary source of the theoretical frameworks underlying AI development, has historically defined intelligence in terms of abstract reasoning, verbal facility, logical processing, and individual problem-solving. These are not universal attributes of intelligence; they are particular emphases that reflect specific educational traditions, testing cultures, and epistemological frameworks.

Howard Gardner's theory of multiple intelligences, developed in the 1980s, documented eight distinct forms of human capability (linguistic, logical-mathematical, spatial, bodily-kinaesthetic, musical, interpersonal, intrapersonal, and naturalistic), most of which standard AI systems neither measure nor value. The AI systems that screen job applicants, assess students, and evaluate creative work overwhelmingly prioritise the subset of capabilities that tests can measure and English-language training data can represent.

This is not merely an academic concern. When AI systems used for talent identification in schools are built on a narrow cognitive model, they consistently miss children who are highly capable in domains the system does not measure. This affects children from all backgrounds, but it disproportionately affects children from communities whose forms of intelligence are furthest from the Western academic model.

The problem extends to who is identified as a potential technology professional. Studies of AI-assisted identification of 'STEM talent' in schools find striking patterns: the children identified as future engineers and programmers cluster heavily among those who resemble the demographic profile of current engineers and programmers. The AI has learned that people who look like software developers tend to become software developers. It is finding a pattern. The pattern reflects prior exclusion, not prior aptitude.

THE EPISTEMOLOGICAL MONOCULTURE

Beyond demographics and definitions of intelligence lies a deeper problem: the epistemological monoculture in AI development. Most AI researchers were trained in the same methodological tradition, read the same journals, attended the same conferences, and shared the same assumptions about what constitutes valid knowledge.

This monoculture has real consequences for what AI systems can represent. Scientific knowledge (peer-reviewed, quantified, replicable) is legible to AI systems trained on academic literature. Traditional knowledge, accumulated through generations of observation and practice but transmitted orally or through apprenticeship, not publication, is largely invisible.

The consequences are most acute in domains where traditional knowledge is not merely alternative but often superior. Traditional ecological knowledge accumulated by communities living in specific landscapes over centuries contains information about local conditions, seasonal variation, and long-term trends that scientific research, which is typically of shorter duration and broader scope, simply cannot replicate. Indigenous fire management practices in Australia, dismissed for decades by Western forestry science as unscientific, are now recognised as sophisticated ecological interventions that produce substantially better outcomes than European-derived approaches. None of this traditional knowledge is routinely integrated into AI systems for land management.

This is not an argument against science. It is an argument that restricting AI's knowledge base to what is in the scientific literature is an epistemological choice with consequences, and that those consequences fall disproportionately on communities whose knowledge is not in the literature.

4

INDIGENOUS WISDOM MEETS SILICON VALLEY

The collision between indigenous knowledge systems and Silicon Valley's technological universalism reveals fundamental incompatibilities in how different cultures perceive intelligence, knowledge, and the appropriate use of technology. This is not a clash between primitive and advanced thinking. It is a confrontation between different but equally sophisticated approaches to understanding and organising the world.

DATA SOVEREIGNTY AND SACRED KNOWLEDGE

Māori data sovereignty frameworks challenge every assumption underlying Western AI development.[56] Where Silicon Valley treats data as raw material for extraction and processing, Māori frameworks view information as *taonga*, treasured possessions that carry ancestral obligations extending across generations.

This distinction is not an abstract philosophical point but a practical governance issue with profound implications for AI development. When New Zealand's health system began implementing AI-driven diagnostic tools, Māori leaders demanded more than consultation. They required fundamental restructuring of how health data was collected, stored, and used. The result was an approach to AI governance that treats data as a living entity with its own rights and relationships. An inert resource for algorithmic consumption, it is not.

The Māori concept of *whakapapa*, genealogical connections that link all things, transforms the way AI systems handle information. Data does not exist in isolation but carries relationships to people, places, and purposes that must be respected. An individual's health data is connected to their family's wellbeing, their tribe's future, and their ancestors' legacy. AI systems that treat this data as individual records for optimisation violate fundamental principles of interconnection.

New Zealand's health system now incorporates these principles through innovative governance structures. Health AI systems must demonstrate how they serve collective wellbeing, not just individual health optimisation.[57] Data use requires collective consent from *iwi* (tribal) representatives, not just individual agreement. Algorithms must be interpretable not just technically but culturally, explaining their decisions in terms that align with Māori concepts of health and healing.

Australian Aboriginal communities have developed similar frameworks that challenge Western assumptions about knowledge ownership. The Arrernte people of Central Australia require that any AI system processing their cultural information include traditional knowledge holders in governance structures.[58] This is not a token representation but a fundamental power-sharing that recognises indigenous authority over indigenous knowledge.

The Arrernte approach reveals how indigenous data sovereignty challenges the technological infrastructure of AI itself. Western AI systems assume centralised data storage, universal access protocols, and standardised processing methods. Arrernte data governance requires distributed control, restricted access based on cultural protocols (some knowledge is only for initiated members, some only for women, some only for elders), and processing methods that respect sacred boundaries.

When an Australian agricultural company sought to use AI to optimise cattle grazing on traditional lands, Arrernte elders did not just negotiate terms of use. They restructured the entire system. The AI could not access sacred sites, even in satellite imagery, and could not process information during ceremony times. It had to incorporate traditional ecological knowledge as equal to scientific data. The resulting system was more complex but also more effective, combining millennia of observation with modern technology in ways that neither could achieve alone.

The Ubuntu philosophy, rooted in the southern African concept that personhood is constituted through relationship with others, provides an alternative perspective that reshapes AI's purpose and role. South African researchers have proposed AI systems designed around collective flourishing.[59] Individual optimisation is not the objective. Their prototype healthcare AI considers not only patient outcomes but also the impacts on families and communities, measuring success through collective well-being.

TRADITIONAL KNOWLEDGE AND MACHINE LEARNING

Indigenous communities worldwide possess sophisticated pattern recognition systems developed over millennia. These knowledge systems offer alternative models for artificial intelligence that Silicon Valley's narrow approach overlooks. The tragedy is not just that indigenous knowledge is ignored. It is that AI systems are actively destroying knowledge systems that could inform better approaches to artificial intelligence itself.

Traditional ecological knowledge demonstrates this vividly. Inuit hunters read ice conditions through subtle cues that satellite monitoring misses.[60] They recognise patterns in wind, current, and animal behaviour that predict ice stability weeks in advance. The integration of indigenous ecological knowledge with Western climate models does not just add data. It creates entirely new ways of understanding climate systems.

An Inuit elder described the difference: 'Your computers see numbers: temperature, pressure, salinity. We see stories: how the ice speaks, what the seals remember, when the winds argue. You predict with mathematics; we predict with relationships. Both work, but together they see what neither sees alone.'

Brazilian indigenous communities' forest management practices, initially dismissed by agricultural AI as 'unproductive,' prove more sustainable and profitable in the long term than algorithmic optimisation.[61] The communities maintain crop diversity that appears inefficient to algorithms trained on monoculture data but provides resilience against climate variation that monocultures lack.

The Kayapó people of the Amazon practise agriculture that Western AI cannot even recognise as farming. They create forest islands, carefully managed ecosystems that concentrate useful plants while maintaining ecological relationships. To satellite imagery and agricultural AI, these look like natural forests. For the Kayapó, they are sophisticated agrarian systems that simultaneously produce food, medicine, materials, and ecological services.

The Kayapó Indigenous Territory forms part of a continuous 28-million-hectare forest corridor in southeastern Amazonia, one of the best-preserved areas in the region.[62] The AI classified sustainable abundance as unproductive wilderness because it could not recognise agriculture that did not look like industrial farming.

Aboriginal Australian fire management provides another example of sophisticated pattern recognition that AI systems fail to recognise. Indigenous Australians have used controlled burning for approximately 50,000 years to manage landscapes, prevent catastrophic wildfires, and maintain ecological diversity.[63] Their burning patterns follow complex protocols based on plant phenology, animal breeding cycles, weather patterns, and spiritual calendars.

Research consistently shows that *restoring* Indigenous fire management reduces the extent of late-dry-season wildfires. WWF-Australia research and studies of the West Arnhem Land Fire Abatement project confirm that reinstating Indigenous burning practices reduced late-season wildfire extent across 115,000 km^2 in northern Australia.[64] Displacing these practices, whether by colonial land management or algorithmic fire suppression systems that treat all fires as threats, entails real ecological losses that Western land management has struggled to reverse.

ALTERNATIVE METRICS FOR SUCCESS

Indigenous and non-Western frameworks propose fundamentally different metrics for evaluating AI success, moving beyond efficiency, accuracy, and profit to consider community wellbeing, cultural sustainability, and long-term impact.

Seven-generation thinking, rooted in the traditions of indigenous North Americans, evaluates decisions based on their impact seven generations into the future.[65] This framework would radically transform AI development, prioritising long-term sustainability over short-term optimisation. An AI system that increases efficiency today but depletes resources for future generations would be considered a failure.

The Haudenosaunee Confederacy, the political union of six indigenous nations of northeastern North America, also known as the Iroquois Confederacy, has practised seven-generation governance for centuries. A Mohawk elder on the Haudenosaunee Grand Council described the contrast: 'Your algorithms think in microseconds, your businesses think in quarters, your governments think in election cycles. We think in centuries. This is why your artificial intelligence creates problems faster than it solves them. It cannot see the future it is creating.'

Gross National Happiness, introduced by Bhutan, offers an alternative metric framework. Instead of measuring economic growth, Bhutan evaluates development in terms of psychological well-being, health, education, cultural diversity, and ecological resilience.[66] AI systems evaluated through this framework would be assessed on whether they increased life satisfaction, not just productivity.

Bhutan's approach to technology adoption demonstrates this in practice. The country rejected certain agricultural AI systems that would increase crop yields but reduce farmer autonomy and satisfaction. They chose educational technology that preserved traditional teaching relationships over more efficient automated instruction. Internet expansion was deliberately slowed to prevent cultural disruption, despite economic costs.

Pacific Island nations have developed climate resilience metrics that evaluate technology on its capacity to adapt, not mitigation statistics.[67] These frameworks assess whether AI systems help communities adapt to unavoidable change. Kiribati, facing imminent submersion due to sea level rise, evaluates technology through the lens of 'migration with dignity', whether systems help communities relocate while maintaining their cultural identity.[68] Agricultural AI that increases food production on islands that will be underwater in decades is less valuable than systems that help communities maintain cultural practices in new locations.

The Marshall Islands measures AI success partly through the preservation of navigational knowledge, traditional wayfinding techniques that allowed Pacific peoples to traverse vast ocean distances without instruments.[69] Educational AI that maintains this knowledge while teaching modern skills is valued over systems that achieve higher test scores through cultural erasure.

These Pacific frameworks recognise that efficiency in dying systems is less valuable than resilience for uncertain futures. AI that optimises current conditions while diminishing the ability to adapt is seen as detrimental, whatever its short-term advantages.

WHEN THE MAP EATS THE TERRITORY

There is a particular hazard in bringing AI to indigenous contexts that practitioners have begun to name: the risk that the process of digitising and encoding indigenous knowledge destroys or distorts the very knowledge it claims to preserve.

Indigenous knowledge systems are typically embedded in practice, relationships, and place. They are not just information. They are ways of knowing that require particular contexts to remain alive and meaningful. A plant's medicinal properties are not separable from the knowledge of when to harvest it, which person in the community holds the right to harvest it, what protocols surround its use, and what obligations accompany receiving it. Entering the chemical compound in a database captures a fragment; the database entry cannot replicate the knowledge system.

This is not a reason to avoid digitising indigenous knowledge. Communities face the very real risk of knowledge loss as elders die and transmission chains break. It is a reason to approach digitisation with humility about what is and is not being preserved, and to ensure that communities retain governance over what has been digitised and the terms on which it may be accessed.

Several indigenous communities have developed what are called 'cultural firewalls' in digital archives: metadata systems that mark certain knowledge as restricted to specific community members, available only at certain times or under certain conditions. This replicates, in digital form, the governance structures that have always surrounded the knowledge. AI systems that access these archives must respect these restrictions, which requires that the AI governance infrastructure encode and enforce cultural access protocols, not merely translate knowledge into an accessible format.

The challenge is that this kind of nuanced, condition-dependent access control is technically demanding and commercially unattractive. Most digital archiving systems are built for open access with occasional restrictions, not for the complex, layered, context-dependent access structures that indigenous knowledge governance requires. Building the technical infrastructure to support genuine indigenous data sovereignty in AI systems requires sustained investment that the market, absent policy requirements, will not make.

TWO-EYED SEEING IN PRACTICE

The Mi'kmaw Elder Albert Marshall developed the concept of *Etuaptmumk*, Two-Eyed Seeing, to describe an approach to knowledge that draws on both indigenous and Western ways of knowing without reducing one to the other or claiming that one is superior.

Two-Eyed Seeing has been applied in healthcare, environmental management, and education across Canada and internationally. Its application to AI development is more recent and less developed, but the principle is clear: systems that genuinely draw on multiple knowledge traditions, treating none as supplementary data for a primary system, are better able to serve the full diversity of human situations.

In practice, Two-Eyed Seeing in AI development requires institutional structures that give indigenous knowledge holders genuine authority alongside technical specialists, not merely advisory roles. It requires that indigenous-language concepts be encoded in ways that preserve their meaning, rather than being forced into English categories through translation. It requires that success be evaluated by the communities the system serves, not only by technical metrics defined by developers.

These requirements are challenging. They are also the minimum necessary for AI systems that claim to serve indigenous communities to actually do so. Performing the appearance of service is not enough.

5

GENDER IN THE MACHINE

Gender bias in AI extends beyond simple discrimination to embed fundamental assumptions about intelligence, capability, and social roles. These systems do not just disadvantage women. They encode particular versions of gender that become computational reality, shaping how society understands and performs gender through algorithmic mediation.

BEYOND BINARY BIAS

Most discussions of gender bias in AI focus on male-female discrimination, overlooking how these systems enforce gender binaries that erase non-binary and transgender identities. This is not just exclusion. It is existential negation, systems that literally cannot conceive of gender beyond binary classification.

Facial recognition systems demonstrate this starkly. Most commercial facial recognition systems include gender classification as a core feature, but these systems recognise only 'male' or 'female.'[70] Non-binary individuals do not just get misclassified. They break the system's fundamental assumptions about human categorisation. The algorithm forces everyone into binary boxes, regardless of their actual identity.

The technical architecture of gender classification reveals deep assumptions. These systems identify gender through facial features that correlate with testosterone or oestrogen exposure: jaw shape, brow prominence, cheekbone structure. But gender is not determined by bone structure, and many people's faces do not conform to binary expectations. The AI is not recognising gender. It is enforcing a particular biological definition of gender that many societies have moved beyond.

When non-binary individuals interact with these systems, they face constant algorithmic friction. Airport security AI that segregates travellers by binary gender forces non-binary people to choose categories that do not represent them. Healthcare AI that provides different recommendations based on binary gender classification gives inappropriate medical advice to people whose bodies do not conform to binary assumptions.

A non-binary software engineer described the experience: 'Every AI interaction becomes a moment of erasure. The system looks at me and says, "You don't exist." I have to choose between misrepresenting myself or being excluded from services. The algorithm doesn't just discriminate against me. It denies my existence.'

Transgender individuals face different but related challenges. Healthcare AI trained on cisgender medical data provides dangerous recommendations for transgender patients.[71] Hormone therapy disrupts the gendered medical patterns these systems expect, leading to misdiagnosis and inappropriate treatment recommendations.

A transgender woman reported that medical AI consistently flagged her hormone levels as 'abnormal' and recommended discontinuing medication that was keeping her alive. The system had learned that specific hormone patterns in people classified as male at birth indicated disease, unable to recognise that she was healthy within transgender parameters. The AI's binary medical model literally pathologised her existence.

Financial AI demonstrates similar binary enforcement. Credit scoring algorithms flag name changes associated with gender transition as indicators of fraud.[72] The systems have learned that name changes correlate with identity theft, and are unable to distinguish between criminal activity and legal gender recognition. Transgender individuals face financial penalties for social transition, with algorithms reducing their credit scores during the most economically vulnerable period of their lives.

GENDERED INTELLIGENCE

AI systems consistently devalue forms of intelligence traditionally associated with femininity: emotional perception, collaborative problem-solving, contextual thinking. This is not accidental but architectural, embedded in how these systems define and measure intelligence.

Performance evaluation AI privileges quantifiable individual achievements over collaborative successes that are difficult to measure.[73] A software engineer who mentors colleagues, builds team cohesion, and prevents conflicts scores lower than one who writes marginally more code but damages team dynamics. The algorithm has learned that productivity is measured by individual output. Collective capability is not in its vocabulary.

The bias extends to how AI systems evaluate communication. Natural language processing trained on corporate communication rates direct, assertive language as 'leadership material' while interpreting collaborative, consensus-building language as 'lacking authority.'[74] Women who communicate in ways that build agreement, and do not issue commands, are algorithmically classified as less capable leaders.

Research has found that AI systems trained on historical text replicate gendered evaluative patterns, rating language coded as masculine more highly in professional contexts.[75] Proposals using competitive, individualistic, quantitative language scored higher than those using collaborative, qualitative language, even when the content was identical. Women entrepreneurs seeking funding through AI-evaluated platforms receive lower scores, not because their businesses are weaker, but because they describe them differently.

Educational AI similarly privileges competitive over collaborative learning. Systems designed to identify 'gifted' students consistently overlook those who excel through peer support and collective problem-solving.[76] Girls who exhibited collaborative learning styles (helping peers, building study groups, sharing knowledge) were consistently tracked into less advanced programmes than boys with identical test scores but competitive learning styles. The AI interpreted collaboration as a need for support. It is a sophisticated learning strategy; the algorithm could not tell the difference.

Even creative AI exhibits gendered patterns. Image generation systems trained on art history produce 'masterpieces' that overwhelmingly reflect male artistic styles while treating women's artistic traditions as deviations.[77] The AI has not learned universal aesthetics. It has learned masculine artistic values and treated them as defaults.

Female artists using AI tools report having to 'masculinise' their prompts to get desired results. Requesting 'powerful' art produces war scenes; they must specify 'powerful tenderness' to get maternal imagery. Asking for 'professional' photography generates men in suits; they must add 'female' to get women, implicitly accepting that 'professional' defaults to male.

THE MOTHERHOOD PENALTY IN ALGORITHMIC SYSTEMS

Employment-related AI systems encode and amplify the motherhood penalty, the systematic disadvantaging of mothers in workplace contexts. These systems do not just reflect existing discrimination; they transform it into mathematical rules that become harder to challenge because they appear objective and impartial.

Performance evaluation AI penalises career patterns associated with motherhood (employment gaps, part-time work, flexible scheduling) interpreting them as reduced commitment.[78] The algorithms learn from historical data where mothers advanced more slowly, without recognising that the slower advancement reflected discrimination, not underperformance.

A multinational corporation's AI evaluation system consistently rated mothers lower than childless women with identical productivity metrics.[79] An investigation revealed that the algorithm was using proxy variables: email response time (mothers could not answer emails during school runs), meeting attendance (mothers missed evening meetings for childcare), and 'visibility' metrics (mothers worked efficiently during school hours and left on time, rather than performatively staying late). The system created cascading discrimination. Lower performance ratings meant smaller raises, reduced bonuses, and fewer opportunities for advancement.

Scheduling AI amplifies motherhood penalties through 'optimisation' that ignores caregiving responsibilities. These systems schedule important meetings during school pickup times, assign travel during school holidays, and allocate projects requiring evening work to 'available' employees, availability defined as absence of caregiving responsibilities.[80]

A mother in tech described the algorithmic discrimination: 'The scheduling AI consistently gave me the worst projects: ones with bad timing, limited resources, or low visibility. It had learned that I couldn't travel frequently or work weekends, so it assigned me work that didn't "require" these things. But those were also the projects that didn't lead to promotion. The algorithm created a mommy track without any human making that discriminatory decision.'

Recruitment AI perpetuates motherhood penalties from the start. Research has found that AI hiring algorithms consistently rank parents lower, regardless of qualifications.[81] Systems trained on successful employee profiles learn to identify 'commitment signals' that correlate with being childless: conference attendance, publication records, continuous employment, and geographic flexibility. Mothers returning to work after parental leave are algorithmically classified as risks before they have had a chance to demonstrate otherwise.

GENDERED DATA AND INVISIBLE WOMEN

The gender bias in AI systems is partly a data problem, partly a design problem, and partly a problem of who decides what counts as a problem in the first place.

The data problem is foundational. Training datasets reflect the world as it has been recorded, not as it is. Women's contributions to history, science, literature, and public life have been consistently underrepresented in the written record. Women were excluded from formal institutions. Their work was attributed to others or went undocumented. When AI systems learn from the historical record, they learn a world in which women are less present, less authoritative, and less central than men.

Caroline Criado Perez documented this problem in *Invisible Women* (2019), demonstrating that the gender data gap affects medical research, crash test dummies, smartphone sizes, office temperature settings, and city planning. AI systems trained on data built from these gender-blind sources inherit and amplify the problem.

The medical data gap is particularly consequential. Clinical trials have historically enrolled predominantly male subjects, on the grounds that female hormonal variation complicates research. The AI systems trained on this research learn normal ranges, dosing guidelines, and symptom presentations from predominantly male data. When they are deployed to serve patients of all genders, their outputs are calibrated to a male baseline.

Heart disease presentation in women is the most studied example: women's symptoms more frequently include fatigue, nausea, and jaw pain; the 'classic' chest pain is a male presentation. An AI diagnostic system trained predominantly on male symptom data will perform worse on female patients, not through any programmed bias but through the faithful reproduction of a gender-blind training set.

THE INTERSECTIONALITY PROBLEM

Gender bias in AI does not operate in isolation. It intersects with racial bias, class bias, disability bias, and every other axis of social inequality in ways that produce compounding disadvantages.

Black women face the intersection of racial and gender bias in AI systems, with effects that cannot be predicted by considering racial bias and gender bias separately. The concept of intersectionality, developed by legal scholar Kimberlé Crenshaw to describe the situation of Black women who fell between categories designed for either race or gender alone, applies with precision to algorithmic discrimination.

The Gender Shades study's finding was not just that AI face recognition was worse for women than men, or worse for darker-skinned people than lighter-skinned people. It was that darker-skinned women faced the worst performance of any group, substantially worse than would be predicted by combining the gender gap and the skin tone gap. The system was not merely performing two kinds of bias in parallel; it had learned a compounded failure mode for the group it encountered least in training.

This has governance implications that most regulatory frameworks have not yet addressed. A regulatory requirement that AI systems demonstrate equal performance across gender categories would not catch intersectional failures if the gender comparison is made within a population that is itself racially homogeneous. Adequate bias testing for intersectional discrimination requires testing across the combinations of protected characteristics, not just each characteristic independently, a substantially more demanding requirement that most current standards do not impose.

PART II

CULTURAL ALGORITHMS, EAST MEETS WEST

6

LOST IN TRANSLATION: AI ACROSS CULTURES

A major American AI company's presentation to Japanese banking executives in Tokyo should have been straightforward. Their customer service chatbot boasted 94% accuracy on English-language benchmarks, with impressive metrics for query resolution, customer satisfaction, and operational efficiency. The demonstration proved catastrophic.

When Japanese customers expressed dissatisfaction through indirect language, 'Perhaps there might be a small issue with my account', the chatbot responded cheerfully: 'Great! I'm glad everything is working perfectly!' The Americans were baffled by the polite but firm rejection. Their algorithm had achieved technical excellence, yet completely misunderstood how communication works in high-context cultures.[82]

This exemplifies AI's translation problem: not just converting languages but working across fundamentally different frameworks for communication, decision-making, and social interaction. The challenge goes far beyond linguistic translation, encompassing entire worldviews embedded in cultural communication patterns that resist algorithmic interpretation.

HIGH-CONTEXT CULTURES AND LOW-CONTEXT MACHINES

Anthropologist Edward T. Hall's distinction between high and low-context cultures illuminates why Western AI consistently fails globally.[83] Low-context cultures (the United States, Germany, the Netherlands) emphasise explicit communication, meaning conveyed through words. High-context cultures (Japan, Korea, Saudi Arabia, Peru) communicate through implications, relationships, and context.

Most AI systems are irredeemably low-context, designed by and for people who expect direct statements. These systems interpret politeness as satisfaction, indirection as confusion, and contextual communication as noise. The mismatch creates not just miscommunication but a fundamental misunderstanding of human intent and meaning.

Korean customer service demonstrates this vividly. When customers say 'Thank you for your help, but...', they are expressing frustration through formulaic courtesy.[84] Western-trained chatbots focus on the gratitude, missing the critique entirely. The AI responds to words, not meaning. This is not poor natural language processing. It is cultural illiteracy encoded in mathematics.

Contract analysis AI trained on Anglo-American legal documents catastrophically misinterprets Middle Eastern contracts that embed meaning in relationship history.[85] Explicit clauses are not the point. A single Arabic phrase might invoke decades of precedent invisible to algorithmic analysis. The phrase 'as we have previously agreed' does not refer to documented agreements but to complex webs of honour, obligation, and reciprocity that exist outside written records.

In the UAE, a Western law firm's contract analysis AI recommended rejecting a billion-dollar infrastructure deal because the contract appeared 'vague' and 'lacked specific performance metrics.'[86] Local lawyers recognised the contract as sound within the cultural context, the foreign partners' reputation and relationships with government officials provided stronger guarantees than any written clause. The AI's inability to recognise social capital as a contractual force nearly destroyed a significant partnership.

Medical consultation AI reveals life-threatening misunderstandings. In Thailand, patients describing pain through metaphor and social context receive algorithmic responses addressing literal interpretations.[87] 'My heart is heavy' triggers cardiac protocols. Depression expressed through cultural idiom does not register. The mistranslation is not just inconvenient. It is potentially fatal when emotional distress gets treated as cardiac disease while actual heart conditions expressed through indirect language get missed.

Japanese business negotiation reveals another dimension of high-context failure. AI systems analysing negotiation transcripts consistently misinterpret Japanese responses.[88] 'That would be difficult' means 'absolutely not.' 'We will consider it' means 'no.' It's interesting' means 'we have concerns.' The AI, trained on American directness, interprets these as positive engagement. They are polite rejections.

A Silicon Valley startup lost a significant partnership when its AI-powered negotiation assistant advised pushing harder after receiving multiple 'we will study this carefully' responses.[89] In Japanese business culture, this phrase signals that the proposal is unacceptable, but the relationship is valued enough to avoid a direct rejection. The AI's interpretation of genuine consideration led to aggressive follow-up, violating cultural norms and destroying trust.

RELIGIOUS FRAMEWORKS AND SECULAR ASSUMPTIONS

AI systems often embed secular Western assumptions that conflict with the religious worldviews that govern most of humanity's decisions. These conflicts are not edge cases. They are fundamental incompatibilities that render AI systems not just ineffective but actively harmful in religious contexts.

In Islamic finance, transactions involving interest (*riba*) are prohibited, as are those with excessive uncertainty (*gharar*) and investments in industries considered *haram*. Financial AI trained on conventional banking recommends precisely what Islamic law forbids. The conflict is not technical but theological. The algorithm optimises for returns that believers consider spiritually destructive.

The prohibition on *riba* is not simply about avoiding interest. It reflects a complete restructuring of financial relationships around profit-sharing. Debt is the problem, not a neutral instrument. Islamic finance employs complex instruments such as *murabaha* (cost-plus financing) and *musharaka* (joint venture), which Western-trained AI systems often classify as 'inefficient' or 'risky' because they do not conform to conventional financial models.

When a major bank deployed Western-developed AI for Islamic banking in Malaysia, the system consistently recommended *haram* investments disguised through complex derivatives.[90] The AI had learned to recognise patterns that maximised returns without understanding that certain returns, regardless of magnitude, were spiritually unacceptable. Muslim customers abandoned the bank in droves, not because the AI performed poorly but because it violated religious principles.

Buddhist principles of non-harm create different conflicts. Agricultural AI recommending pesticides violates *ahimsa* principles that many farmers consider more important than yield optimisation.[91] The system's economic logic confronts spiritual priorities that it cannot comprehend. Thai Buddhist farmers report that following AI agricultural recommendations causes spiritual distress that manifests as physical illness, community discord, and agricultural failure, outcomes the AI cannot predict because it cannot recognise spiritual variables.

A Buddhist monk advising farmers in Sri Lanka described the problem: 'The AI tells us to poison the earth for a better harvest. But the earth remembers violence. The insects we kill return as plant disease. The soil we dose with chemicals becomes barren. The AI sees only this season's yield, not the karma we create for generations.'

Hindu concepts of auspicious timing affect everything from medical procedures to business launches. Scheduling AI that ignores *muhurat* (astrologically favourable moments) creates systems that users consider fundamentally unlucky.[92] A Mumbai hospital found that surgical outcomes appeared to improve when procedures were scheduled according to traditional Hindu timing, not AI optimisation: whether reflecting spiritual reality or the psychological effects of patient and staff beliefs, the outcome was real: ignoring religious timing requirements increased perceived and actual medical risk.

Indigenous spiritual frameworks present even more complex challenges. Many indigenous cultures recognise non-human entities (spirits, ancestors, land) as stakeholders in decision-making. AI systems that process only human input exclude entities that indigenous communities consider essential participants.

Australian Aboriginal communities rejected a land management AI system that optimised resource extraction without consulting country.[93] From a Western perspective, 'country' is a geographic area. From the Aboriginal perspective, country is a living entity with its own interests, knowledge, and requirements. The AI's inability to recognise non-human stakeholders made its recommendations not just inappropriate but sacrilegious.

COLLECTIVE DECISION-MAKING VERSUS INDIVIDUAL OPTIMISATION

Western AI assumes individual users making autonomous decisions. This framework fails catastrophically in cultures where decisions emerge through collective deliberation. It is not just a different decision-making style. It is a fundamentally different understanding of human agency and social existence.

In Senegal, healthcare decisions often involve extended family consultation, guidance from elders, and community input.[94] Medical AI providing personalised recommendations to individual patients undermines traditional decision-making structures. The technology's efficiency becomes socially destructive, fragmenting healthcare choices that should unite families.

A Senegalese family described their experience with AI-driven healthcare: 'The machine told my daughter she needed surgery. It sent the message to her phone, not to the family. She was terrified, alone with this knowledge. In our culture, medical decisions are made in collaboration. The family must agree, the elders must approve, and the community must support. The AI broke our unity, created secrets where there should be sharing.'

Indonesian communities make financial decisions through *musyawarah*, an extended consultation that reaches consensus.[95] Instant loan approval algorithms bypass this deliberative process, creating debt without community agreement. What appears as financial inclusion becomes social exclusion when technology overrides cultural governance.

A Javanese village elder described the destruction caused by instant loan apps: 'Before, when someone needed money, the village met. We discussed their need, our resources, and what we could share. The debt belonged to all of us. Now the phone gives money instantly, secretly. People have debts we don't know about and can't help with. Families discover bankruptcy when it's too late. The machine broke our economy of sharing.'

Chinese families coordinate educational decisions across three generations, balancing individual aptitude with family needs.[96] Educational AI recommending career paths based on personal interest ignores collective considerations that families weigh more heavily. A Chinese grandmother described the conflict: 'The machine told her to study art because she's talented. But who will continue the family business? Who will care for us when we're old? The machine thinks she is alone in the world, but she is part of a family with obligations and support.'

Pacific Island communities demonstrate even more complex collective decision-making. In Fiji, the *vanua* (community) encompasses not only living humans but also their ancestors, future generations, and the land itself.[97] Decisions must serve all these stakeholders simultaneously. AI systems that optimise for current human benefit violate obligations to ancestors and descendants.

A Fijian chief described why his community rejected AI-optimised fishing quotas: 'The machine says we can take more fish sustainably. But our ancestors established relationships with the reef. Our grandchildren will inherit those relationships. The fish are family, not resources. The AI counts fish but cannot see relationships. Its efficiency is our spiritual poverty.'

ECONOMIC AND SOCIAL STATUS ASSUMPTIONS

AI systems developed in affluent Western contexts embed assumptions about economic resources, social mobility, and lifestyle choices that render their recommendations not just irrelevant but actively harmful in other economic contexts.

Consumer recommendation AI assumes disposable income, consumer choice, and market access that do not exist for most of humanity. In Bangladesh, an e-commerce AI consistently recommended products that cost more than users' monthly income.[98] The system had been trained on data from wealthy countries where such purchases might require saving, but remained possible. For Bangladeshi users, the recommendations were not aspirational but insulting, constant reminders of global inequality encoded in algorithmic assumptions.

Career guidance AI reveals similar economic blindness. Systems trained in contexts with strong labour markets, social safety nets, and educational financing recommend career paths impossible in other financial realities. A career counselling AI deployed in Manila public schools consistently recommended overseas education and international careers.[99] The system could not comprehend that most students could not afford a local university, let alone an international education.

Housing AI demonstrates the violence of misplaced economic assumptions. In Mumbai slums, an AI system advising tenants to 'document everything' and 'know your rights' led to evictions.[100] Slumlords often disregard legal processes; asserting rights that exist on paper but not in practice can label tenants as troublemakers, leading to expulsion.

Dating and social applications designed for Western relationship patterns become dangerous in cultures with different courtship traditions. In Pakistan, a dating app's AI encouraged women to 'be bold' and 'take initiative' in romantic pursuits.[101] Several women who followed this advice faced violent retaliation from families who viewed their behaviour as bringing shame. The AI could not comprehend that dating advice that is liberating in San Francisco could be life-threatening in Peshawar.

An Egyptian woman described how a professional networking site's AI posting recommendations damaged her life: 'It kept suggesting I share my professional achievements, post about my work, and build my personal brand. I followed the advice. My posts were professional, modest, and appropriate. But my family was horrified. A woman's public self-promotion brought shame. My engagement was broken. My brothers stopped speaking to me. The AI's career advice destroyed my life.'

7

THE ASIAN APPROACH TO ARTIFICIAL INTELLIGENCE

Asian AI development reflects philosophical traditions, governance models, and social priorities that diverge fundamentally from Western frameworks. This is not a technological lag but an intentional difference. AI is designed for collective harmony, social stability, and long-term sustainability. Individual optimisation, disruption, and short-term profit are not the objectives.

SINGAPORE'S CALIBRATED INNOVATION

Singapore exemplifies pragmatic AI governance, striking a balance between innovation and social stability through careful calibration.[102] The city-state views AI as critical infrastructure requiring systematic integration, not a disruptive force to be urgently responded to or left to market dynamics.

Singapore's Model AI Governance Framework embodies this calibrated approach through sector-specific adaptation, not universal rules.[103] Healthcare AI faces different requirements from financial AI, recognising that universal standards serve neither innovation nor protection. This modularity enables rapid deployment while maintaining oversight, achieving a balance that Western frameworks struggle to maintain.

The framework operates through collaboration, not regulatory command. Government agencies, industry partners, research institutions, and civil society cooperate in developing AI applications that serve national priorities while respecting social boundaries. This is neither the adversarial relationship between regulators and industry common in the West, nor the state command seen in China, but cooperative governance that aligns diverse stakeholder interests.

Singapore's approach to facial recognition demonstrates calibrated deployment in practice. Rather than ubiquitous surveillance or complete prohibition, the technology operates in specific contexts with transparent limitations.[104] Airport security uses comprehensive facial recognition for border control, a defined national security application with public support. The same technology is restricted in public housing estates, where residents vote on camera installation, balancing security and privacy through democratic deliberation, not technocratic imposition.

The voting process reveals a sophisticated governance design. Residents engage in structured deliberation about specific uses, data retention periods, and oversight mechanisms. The government provides education about capabilities and risks, ensuring informed consent. Manipulation through fear or ignorance is what the process is designed to prevent. Communities that approve surveillance also establish resident committees with real power to audit and modify systems.

The regulatory sandbox model, pioneered in Singapore, enables controlled experimentation with AI that benefits both innovation and governance.[105] Companies test innovations under relaxed requirements while regulators learn about emerging capabilities. A fintech company testing AI-driven micro loans in the sandbox discovered their algorithm discriminated against ethnic minorities, not through intentional bias but through proxy variables correlating with race.[106] Rather than facing penalties, they worked with regulators to identify and eliminate the sources of bias. The collaborative approach achieved fair lending more quickly than either market competition or regulatory enforcement could have accomplished alone.

JAPAN'S HUMAN-CENTRIC INTEGRATION

Japanese AI development prioritises human-machine collaboration over replacement, reflecting cultural values around harmony, respect for human dignity, and preservation of social relationships.[107] This shapes everything from robot design to algorithmic decision-making, creating AI that augments human capabilities without supplanting them.

Toyota's manufacturing AI exemplifies this philosophy through systems that strengthen worker capabilities while preserving employment and expertise.[108] Toyota develops AI that extends the capabilities of human workers; the workers stay. Exoskeletons reduce physical strain without eliminating jobs. Decision support systems improve judgment without removing human authority. Quality control AI identifies problems for human resolution; it does not automatically correct them.

The approach seems inefficient by Western standards focused on labour cost reduction. But Toyota achieves superior quality, worker satisfaction, and innovation through human-AI collaboration that neither alone could accomplish. Workers who train AI systems develop deeper expertise. AI that supports humans maintains institutional knowledge.

A Toyota engineer described the philosophy: 'Americans use AI to eliminate workers. The Chinese use AI to control workers. We use AI to elevate workers. The machine makes humans more human: more creative, more skilled, more valuable. This isn't just kindness. It's also a strategy. Humans and machines together surpass either alone.'

Japan faces acute demographic challenges, including a rapidly ageing population and a shrinking working-age population. Rather than warehousing the elderly in minimal care facilities monitored by

AI, Japan develops robots that preserve dignity while providing assistance.[109] Robotic care assistants do not replace human caregivers but address specific needs while maintaining human connection. Lifting robots prevent injury to caregivers and patients while preserving human touch for comfort. Companion robots provide stimulation and monitoring without replacing family relationships.

Japan's consensus-building tradition shapes AI governance through extensive consultation.[110] New AI systems undergo review not just by regulators but by affected communities, industry associations, and civil society. The consultation process for AI deployment in Japanese schools took three years.[111] Teachers, parents, students, and communities deliberated about appropriate uses, necessary restrictions, and evaluation metrics. The resulting system had lower technical capabilities than alternatives but higher acceptance and effectiveness.

The concept of *ikigai* (life purpose found at the intersection of what you love, what you are good at, what the world needs, and what you can be paid for) influences how Japan evaluates AI success.[112] Systems are assessed not only on efficiency but on whether they help people find meaning and make a contribution. This existential dimension, absent from Western metrics focused on productivity and profit, creates AI serving human flourishing. Economic optimisation is a secondary consideration at best.

A Japanese government official described their AI evaluation framework: 'Western countries measure AI by economic impact: productivity, GDP, profit. China measures stability, compliance, and order. We measure by human development: are people growing, finding purpose, building relationships? The economy serves life, not life serving the economy.'

CHINA'S SOCIETAL ENGINEERING

China approaches AI as infrastructure for social coordination at an unprecedented scale, embedding Confucian values of hierarchy, harmony, and collective prosperity into technological systems.[113] This creates AI that Western observers find troubling, but which operates within different philosophical frameworks regarding the individual versus collective good.

The Social Credit System represents comprehensive behavioural coordination through algorithmic incentives.[114] Western critics focus on surveillance and control, while missing how the system reflects Chinese priorities for social trust and collective responsibility. Citizens with high scores access benefits not as individual rewards, but as recognition of their social contributions.

The system operates through transparent rules that citizens can understand and act on. Unlike Western credit scores, which use opaque algorithms, Chinese social credit publicly reports specific behaviours that increase or decrease scores. Donating blood adds points. Traffic violations subtract them. Helping neighbours adds points. Littering subtracts them. The system makes virtue profitable, creating social pressure for ethical behaviour that informal social control no longer provides in rapidly urbanising China.

A Beijing resident described her perspective: 'Westerners see oppression. We see accountability. In anonymous cities, people misbehave without consequences. The social credit system recreates village social pressure at an urban scale. Everyone knows if you cheat, litter, or fight. This isn't surveillance. It's civilisation.'

China's AI governance emphasises stability over the speed of innovation, carefully testing new systems before widespread deployment.[115] New AI applications undergo trials in designated zones, enabling authorities to identify and address issues before national rollout. This contrasts with Silicon Valley's 'move fast and break things' ethos, prioritising social continuity over technological disruption.

Educational AI in China incorporates moral cultivation alongside academic achievement, reflecting Confucian emphasis on character development.[116] Systems assess student integrity, social contribution, and collective spirit, dimensions that Western educational AI overlooks. Chinese educational AI tracks not just test scores but classroom behaviour, peer relationships, and social contributions.

Students who help struggling classmates receive recognition. Those who excel individually while ignoring collective needs face criticism.

A Shanghai teacher described the philosophy: 'Western education creates competitors, individuals racing against each other. Our AI-supported education creates collaborators, citizens building society together. We measure not just what students know but who they become.'

SOUTH KOREA'S DIGITAL DEMOCRACY

South Korea combines rapid technological advancement with democratic governance, creating unique approaches to AI accountability that treat technology as public infrastructure requiring democratic oversight.[117] This synthesis achieves innovation with accountability and progress through participation.

Seoul's AI governance involves direct citizen participation through digital platforms that extend representative democracy into algorithmic realms.[118] Residents do not just elect representatives who make AI-driven decisions. They directly participate in algorithmic governance through digital democracy tools.

The Seoul Digital Mayor platform enables citizens to audit automated decisions affecting them.[119] If AI denies a permit, citizens can examine the decision-making process, challenge the variables, and demand a human review. Citizens can question why certain factors were weighted, what alternatives were considered, and how decisions align with policy objectives. The platform presents decision logic in clear, accessible language, avoiding technical jargon.

Korean AI development emphasises technological sovereignty: building domestic capabilities.[120] This is not protectionism but strategic autonomy, ensuring that Korean values shape Korean AI. Importing Silicon Valley assumptions or Chinese approaches is not the plan.

The concept of *jeong*, a deep emotional connection that transcends individual relationships, influences Korean social AI design.[121] Systems prioritise maintaining and strengthening social bonds over efficient information exchange. Social media algorithms recommend content that builds community; maximising engagement is not the primary metric. Dating apps optimise for relationship stability, not match quantity.

A Korean AI researcher described the distinction: 'Western AI optimises for individual satisfaction: more engagement, more matches, more connections. Our AI optimises for collective wellbeing: stronger communities, more stable relationships and mutual prosperity. We measure success not by usage metrics but by social cohesion.'

THE CONFUCIAN ROOTS OF COLLECTIVE AI

To understand why East Asian AI development takes different forms across countries, it helps to examine the philosophical tradition they share and the ways they have diverged from it.

Confucian thought, which has shaped the cultural and institutional landscape of China, Japan, Korea, and Vietnam for over two millennia, provides a different starting point for thinking about the relationship between the individual and society than Western liberal philosophy. The Confucian tradition does not begin with the autonomous individual and asks how social institutions can serve individual interests. It begins with the web of relationships (family, community, state) within which individuals are embedded, and asks how individuals can fulfil their roles within those relationships in ways that maintain social harmony.

This is not merely cultural background noise. It produces distinctly different intuitions about what AI systems should do. An AI system designed within a Confucian framework is not primarily a tool for individual self-advancement. It is a social coordination mechanism. Its success is measured not by how well it serves individual preferences but by how well it maintains and strengthens the social fabric.

This difference in starting assumptions produces visible differences in AI product design. Japanese AI systems for customer service are built around harmony preservation; rapid resolution is not the primary goal. Korean AI systems for social media prioritise community cohesion over engagement maximisation. Chinese AI systems for urban management integrate social stability criteria that would not appear in a Western optimisation function.

None of this makes East Asian AI automatically better or worse than Western AI. It differs in specific ways that become clear once you understand the underlying values. It also means that East Asian AI systems, when deployed in Western contexts, can be as culturally alien as Western AI systems are in East Asian contexts.

TECHNOLOGY AND SOCIAL TRUST

One dimension of East Asian AI development that Western analysts frequently misread is the relationship between AI systems and social trust. Western AI ethics discourse tends to treat trust as something AI systems must earn from sceptical users. East Asian AI deployment has more often treated AI systems as trust-building infrastructure, mechanisms through which the state demonstrates its capacity to serve citizens and citizens demonstrate their participation in collective social projects.

This is visible in the public response to AI-enabled public services across East Asian democracies. South Korean and Japanese surveys consistently show higher public confidence in AI-managed public services than European surveys show in equivalent contexts. This is not naive acceptance; both countries have active civil society organisations monitoring AI governance. It reflects a different baseline relationship between citizens and public institutions, in which competent technical management of public services is an expected form of state performance, not a potential threat to individual autonomy.

The implication for AI governance is significant. Governance frameworks transplanted from Western contexts, which tend to frame AI governance primarily as protection of individuals against state or corporate overreach, may fit poorly in contexts where the governance question is primarily about ensuring that AI-mediated state services are delivered fairly and competently. Both framings capture something real. Neither captures everything. A governance framework built to shield individuals from the state, transplanted to a setting where the live question is equitable collective provision, does more than fit badly: it misreads the bias problem itself, recording failures of fair service delivery as though they were violations of individual rights.

8

CONFUCIAN COMPUTING

Confucian philosophy, often misunderstood as ancient traditionalism, offers sophisticated frameworks for AI governance that prioritise social harmony, moral cultivation, and collective flourishing over individual optimisation and competitive disruption. These principles, emerging from 2,500 years of philosophical development, provide alternative approaches to artificial intelligence that challenge Western assumptions about technology's purpose and operation.

THE RECTIFICATION OF NAMES

Confucius began with *zhengming*: ensuring names correspond to reality.[122] This principle profoundly affects AI language processing in Confucian-influenced societies, requiring systems that accurately represent social relationships, use appropriate honourifics, and maintain hierarchical distinctions that Western AI often flattens into false equality.

Chinese customer service AI adjusts communication based on age, social position, and relationship history.[123] A complaint from an elderly customer triggers different protocols than identical feedback from younger users, not discrimination but cultural respect. The algorithm recognises that equality does not mean identical treatment; justice requires treating different situations differently.

The sophistication goes beyond simple age differentiation. The AI considers relationship duration, interaction history, social connections, and contextual information. A long-term customer receives different treatment than a new user. A complaint during the Spring Festival gets a different response than during ordinary times. Every interaction updates the relationship status, affecting future communications. The AI does not just process transactions. It maintains relationships.

Korean AI incorporates *nunchi*: the subtle art of social awareness and situational assessment.[124] Systems detect indirect disagreement, implied criticism, and unspoken expectations that explicit communication misses. *Nunchi* operates through multiple channels simultaneously. Tone carries a different meaning from words. Timing communicates separately from content. Silence speaks as loudly as speech.

Korean systems trained on *nunchi* achieve superior customer satisfaction by recognising and responding to emotional undercurrents that direct communication misses. They detect customer frustration before it escalates, identify satisfaction beyond surface politeness, and read the complex emotional terrain that Western AI blindly stumbles through.

Japanese honourific systems pose a fundamental challenge to AI translation. The difference between *-san*, *-sama*, and *-kun* is not just formality but entire relationship frameworks.[125] Translation AI that renders these as generic 'Mr./Ms.' destroys the meaning embedded in social positioning. The honourific system encodes relative age, social status, relationship type, emotional distance, and contextual appropriateness simultaneously. Using *-chan* with an adult colleague might indicate intimacy or be an insult, depending on context. Japanese AI systems maintain complex models of social relationships that update dynamically, every interaction potentially shifts the relationship parameters.

VIRTUE ETHICS IN ALGORITHMIC DESIGN

Confucian virtue ethics suggests AI should cultivate good character. Simply optimising outcomes is insufficient. This fundamentally reconceptualises algorithmic objectives from efficiency to moral development, from profit to virtue, from optimisation to cultivation.

Chinese social media AI incorporates features that actively promote respectful discourse, ethical reasoning, and social responsibility.[126] Systems do not just moderate content but actively encourage virtuous interaction. Users receive greater visibility for constructive contributions; controversial engagement is not rewarded. The algorithm rewards bridge-building over polarisation, wisdom over wit, kindness over cleverness.

This is not simple sentiment analysis but a sophisticated assessment of virtue. The AI recognises different virtues: *ren* (benevolence) in helping others solve problems; *yi* (righteousness) in defending vulnerable users; *li* (propriety) in maintaining respectful discourse; *zhi* (wisdom) in providing thoughtful analysis; and *xin* (trustworthiness) in sharing accurate information. Users develop virtue scores that affect their influence on the platform.

A Chinese social media executive described the philosophy: 'Western platforms optimise for engagement: anger, outrage, conflict drive clicks. We optimise for harmony: wisdom, kindness, truth build community. Short-term metrics suffer, but long-term value grows. A harmonious platform retains users, attracts advertisers, and serves society.'

Educational AI in Confucian contexts emphasises moral reasoning, social consideration, and ethical development alongside academic content.[127] Chinese educational AI evaluates students across the five constant virtues (*wuchang*): *ren* (benevolence), *yi* (righteousness), *li* (propriety), *zhi* (wisdom), and *xin* (trustworthiness).[128] Academic achievement without virtue development is considered educational failure.

The assessment goes beyond behaviour tracking to the evaluation of moral reasoning. AI presents ethical dilemmas and evaluates responses not for 'correct' answers but for moral sophistication. The system teaches that ethics is not rule-following but thoughtful judgement across complex moral terrain.

Singapore's AI governance requires 'human-centric' design, prioritising social benefits over technical optimisation.[129] This is not empty rhetoric but specific requirements with enforcement mechanisms. AI systems must demonstrate community value, not just technical capability. Does the system strengthen human capability or replace it? Does it strengthen social bonds or fragment them? Does it promote civic virtue or selfish behaviour? Systems that fail these evaluations face restrictions regardless of their technical sophistication or economic value.

HARMONY AS AN OPTIMISATION TARGET

Confucian philosophy prioritises social harmony over individual satisfaction, collective flourishing over personal optimisation. This creates AI systems with fundamentally different objective functions from those of Western algorithms, which focus on engagement, efficiency, or profit.

Chinese urban planning AI optimises for social harmony.[130] Economic efficiency is not the primary target. The system considers not just traffic flow but community cohesion; not just housing density but social stability; not just commercial activity but neighbourhood character. When allocating resources for urban development, AI weighs factors that are invisible to Western planning algorithms. Will this development displace long-term residents? Will it create economic disparities that breed resentment? Will it fragment communities or strengthen them?

A Beijing urban planner described the approach: 'Western cities optimise for efficiency: faster commutes, higher density, maximum land value. We optimise for harmony: stable communities, balanced development, and social cohesion. An efficient city full of strangers is a failure. A less efficient city of neighbours is success.'

Japanese consensus-building AI facilitates group decision-making.[131] The system does not make decisions. It helps groups reach consensus through structured deliberation, information synthesis, and compromise identification. The goal is harmony: reaching decisions that everyone can accept. Optimal solutions that some oppose are no success at all.

Korean conflict resolution AI emphasises face-saving and relationship preservation.[132] Truth-finding and blame assignment are not the objective. The system seeks solutions that allow all parties to maintain dignity. In workplace disputes, the AI suggests resolutions that avoid direct confrontation or explicit admission of fault. Both parties save face while addressing underlying issues. The system recognises that in collectivist cultures, being proven wrong publicly destroys future cooperation.

LONG-TERM THINKING AND INTERGENERATIONAL RESPONSIBILITY

Confucian philosophy emphasises long-term consequences and intergenerational obligations that extend far beyond Western planning horizons. This creates AI systems designed for sustainability and continuity. Disruption and rapid change are not virtues.

Chinese infrastructure AI plans for 50-100 year timeframes.[133] Election cycles and quarterly earnings are not the relevant units of time. When planning high-speed rail networks, the AI considers demographic shifts over decades, climate change over centuries, and cultural preservation over generations. Routes that seem suboptimal today might serve future population centres. Stations placed in empty fields anticipate cities that do not yet exist. The system trades short-term efficiency for long-term adaptability.

Japanese manufacturing AI embodies *monozukuri*: the art of making things with pride, dedication, and continuous improvement.[134] Systems optimise for quality that lasts generations. Planned obsolescence is not a design goal. Toyota's production AI evaluates manufacturing decisions based on 30-year vehicle lifespans, not warranty periods. The system also carefully preserves and transmits expertise across generations, ensuring that retirement does not mean the loss of institutional knowledge.

Korean *chaebols* (family-controlled conglomerates) use AI for succession planning, ensuring business continuity across generations.[135] The systems identify and develop talent not just for immediate needs, but for leadership decades in the future. The AI tracks not just individual performance but family dynamics, educational development, and character formation over decades. Potential successors are identified in childhood, developed through adolescence, and tested through young adulthood.

CONFUCIAN TECHNOLOGY ETHICS IN PRACTICE

The gap between Confucian philosophical principles and the actual deployment of AI in Confucian-influenced societies is substantial and worth acknowledging honestly.

China's social credit system is frequently cited in Western media as a demonstration of Confucian collectivism applied to AI governance, the social fabric made legible and algorithmically enforceable. The reality is more complicated. The social credit system is not a single unified system but a collection of largely sector-specific programmes with different operators, different standards, and different consequences. Its relationship to Confucian ethics is contested: some Chinese scholars argue it represents a genuine attempt to rebuild social trust eroded by rapid economic transformation; others argue it is a technological instrument for political control that appropriates Confucian vocabulary without reflecting Confucian values.

The distinction matters because it bears on how transferable the model is. If the social credit approach reflects genuine Confucian values about social responsibility and collective flourishing, it represents one culturally coherent answer to the governance challenges of algorithmic society. If it primarily reflects the particular interests of a one-party state in monitoring and controlling the population, the Confucian framing is rhetorical decoration.

Japanese AI ethics has developed a more explicitly philosophical body of work exploring what Confucian and Buddhist principles actually require in the context of automated decision-making. The concept of *ningen soncho*, respect for human dignity, as an AI design requirement goes beyond Western notions of individual rights to encompass the relational dimensions of dignity: the importance of how people are treated within their communities, not just whether their individual rights are respected.

Korean AI ethics scholarship has similarly engaged seriously with the question of what distinctly Korean or Confucian values the country's AI development should reflect, beyond the instrumental nationalism of building domestic capability to avoid foreign dependency. The answers remain contested. The engagement is genuine.

THE JAPANESE ROBOTICS LESSON

Japan's experience with service robotics offers a cautionary case study for the broader project of culturally inflected AI development. The country invested heavily in humanoid and eldercare robots on the grounds that Japanese culture's high tolerance for robot-human interaction (compared to Western cultures, where robots trigger uncanny valley discomfort) would support the adoption of robot-assisted care.

The cultural tolerance proved real. Japanese people were indeed more accepting of robot caregivers than their European counterparts. But tolerance did not translate to preference. When given a genuine choice, most Japanese elderly people preferred human carers. The preference for human connection was not merely cultural prejudice against technology; it reflected something that robot interaction genuinely could not provide.

The lesson was that cultural acceptance of a technology and genuine service delivery are different things. Japan's AI and robotics development had successfully calibrated for cultural acceptance while undercalibrating for what the people it was meant to serve actually needed. The adjustment, building robots that genuinely complement human care, required listening more carefully to the people the technology was meant to serve. Cultural tolerance for robots had been assumed to mean satisfaction with robot care. It did not. If a high-trust, culturally aligned programme could mistake tolerance for genuine fit, deployments that are not culturally calibrated at all, the systems shipped from California to Lagos and from Shenzhen to Jakarta, should be treated as carrying that same miscalibration as their baseline condition.

This is a version of the participation problem that appears throughout this book: the people whose lives are most affected by technology decisions need to be in the room where those decisions are made, not as objects of well-intentioned design but as genuine decision-makers. Japanese eldercare robotics eventually moved toward this model. The adjustment could have been made earlier if the starting assumption had been different.

9

THE ASEAN WAY

The conference room in Jakarta was deliberately arranged to avoid hierarchical seating, with a circular table reflecting the Indonesian tradition of *musyawarah mufakat*: consultation for consensus.[136] Representatives from ten different nations had gathered to discuss regional AI governance standards, each bringing distinct cultural perspectives, economic priorities, and technological capabilities.

The contrast with typical Western technology meetings was immediately apparent. Instead of competitive presentations and decisive leadership from dominant players, the conversation meandered through careful consultation, respectful consideration of different viewpoints, and gradual building toward collective understanding. What might appear inefficient to Silicon Valley standards was actually sophisticated consensus-building designed to preserve unity within extraordinary diversity.

MUSYAWARAH MUFAKAT IN ALGORITHM DESIGN

The Indonesian principle of *musyawarah mufakat* influences how Southeast Asian nations approach AI governance: decisions emerge through extended consultation, ensuring all voices are heard.[137] Quick votes and executive mandates are not the ASEAN way. This process takes longer but creates a sustainable agreement that serves diverse interests.

ASEAN adopted its Guide on AI Governance and Ethics in February 2024, the product of regional deliberation that began in earnest around 2019-20.[138] Western observers saw inefficiency; participants saw relationship-building essential for sustainable agreement. The framework's flexibility reflects consensus: principles that everyone accepts, not rules imposed by some on others.

Thai healthcare AI incorporates family consultation features reflecting collective medical decision-making.[139] Systems do not provide instant recommendations but facilitate discussions among patients, families, and traditional healers. Speed surrenders to social process, but outcomes improve through collective buy-in.

The AI presents medical information in formats accessible to different participants. Technical data for doctors, visual explanations for patients, cost analyses for families, and spiritual considerations for traditional healers. Decisions emerge through synthesis. Medical dictation is not the model. This consultative approach achieves superior outcomes despite apparent inefficiency, patients who participate in collective decision-making tend to exhibit better treatment compliance.

Malaysian financial AI accommodates Islamic finance requirements, Chinese business practices, and Indian banking traditions simultaneously.[140] Systems adapt to user cultural contexts; standardisation is not forced. The same underlying AI engine exhibits different interaction patterns in various cultural contexts. Islamic finance modules calculate returns based on profit-sharing, not interest. Chinese business modules emphasise relationship banking and informal credit. Indian modules incorporate family business structures and community lending.

Philippine educational AI switches between English, Filipino, and regional languages within single conversations, recognising that multilingual communication is normal, not exceptional.[141] Students might ask questions in their mother tongue, receive explanations in Filipino, and read technical terms in English, natural code-switching that monolingual AI would find incomprehensible. The system recognises that language choice signals different types of thinking: mother tongue for emotional processing, Filipino for social reasoning, and English for technical analysis.

UNITY IN DIVERSITY AS A DESIGN PRINCIPLE

Unlike Western universalism or Chinese standardisation, ASEAN treats diversity as a fundamental requirement rather than a problem to be solved.[142] AI systems must operate across multiple contexts without imposing a singular framework.

Singapore's national AI systems serve four official languages, multiple ethnic communities, and various religious groups without favouring any particular approach.[143] Government services AI provides culturally appropriate interfaces that go beyond translation to cultural adaptation. For Chinese users, the system emphasises efficiency and family consideration. For Malay users, it incorporates Islamic requirements and community consultation. For Indian users, it accommodates complex family structures and religious diversity.

Indonesian AI for the world's largest archipelago nation accommodates hundreds of ethnic groups without forcing assimilation.[144] The system does not just translate between languages but between worldviews. Javanese indirect communication, Batak directness, Balinese ceremonial formality, Papuan communal decision-making, each receives appropriate accommodation. Indonesian citizenship does not mean Indonesian uniformity; unity does not require homogeneity.

Vietnamese AI development incorporates *doi moi* principles, renovation without abandoning core values.[145] Banking AI modernises financial services while maintaining traditional *hui* (rotating credit associations) that serve communities Western banking ignores. The system formalises informal lending without destroying social relationships that make it work.

Thai AI initiatives preserve cultural traditions while embracing technological advancement.[146] Agricultural AI incorporates royal agricultural theories that emphasise sufficiency economy: moderation, reasonableness, and risk management through diversification.[147] The system does not maximise yield but optimises resilience. Farmers using AI achieve lower peak income but higher sustained wellbeing, fewer bankruptcies, and fewer windfalls.

COLLECTIVE RESILIENCE OVER INDIVIDUAL OPTIMISATION

ASEAN approaches to AI prioritise collective resilience over individual optimisation, recognising that regional stability serves everyone better than a competitive advantage that creates winners and losers.

The ASEAN Smart Cities Network shares AI capabilities.[148] Competing for technological dominance is not the model. Cities collaborate on traffic management, disaster response, and public services, building common infrastructure rather than redundant systems. Singapore's traffic AI helps Jakarta reduce congestion. Bangkok's flood prediction assists Ho Chi Minh City. Kuala Lumpur's crime prevention supports Manila.

ASEAN disaster response AI coordinates across national boundaries, sharing resources and information during emergencies.[149] The system does not optimise for national interest but for regional survival. Resources flow to the greatest need regardless of origin. Information is shared freely despite competitive implications. During disasters, the AI treats ASEAN as a single entity; a regional catastrophe affects everyone regardless of borders.

ASEAN economic AI promotes regional development over

national competition.[150] Systems identify complementary advantages, encouraging specialisation that serves collective prosperity. Singapore focuses on financial AI, Thailand on agricultural AI, the Philippines on service AI, and Vietnam on manufacturing AI. Each develops expertise that serves regional needs; duplicating capabilities across ten countries would serve no one.

THE REGULATION OF AI ACROSS BORDERS

The ASEAN governance model faces its sharpest test in the regulation of AI systems deployed across borders. When a recommendation algorithm built in Singapore shapes content consumed in Indonesia, which country's governance standards apply? When an e-commerce AI developed in Malaysia operates in Vietnam, whose consumer protection framework governs algorithmic pricing?

These are not hypothetical questions. They are live disputes that ASEAN's consensus-based governance architecture was not designed to resolve quickly. The region's digital economy is deeply integrated; its regulatory frameworks remain national. The resulting gap is regularly exploited by platforms that route their algorithmic systems through whichever jurisdiction offers the lightest oversight.

ASEAN's response has been to develop bilateral and multilateral mutual recognition frameworks, bypassing the need for harmonised rules. Two countries agree to recognise each other's AI governance processes as adequate, creating regulatory equivalence without regulatory uniformity. The model mirrors ASEAN's approach to product safety standards: accept each other's certification rather than requiring identical standards.

The limitation of this approach is that mutual recognition requires mutual capacity. Recognition is meaningful only when both parties have genuine technical capacity to conduct the assessments they are recognising. In a region with significant variation in regulatory technical expertise, mutual recognition risks becoming mutual non-enforcement.

Singapore's investment in technical regulatory capacity has positioned it as a de facto hub for ASEAN AI governance. Companies seeking regional deployment often choose Singapore as their primary compliance jurisdiction, on the grounds that Singapore approval signals adequacy to other ASEAN members. This replicates, at a regional scale, a version of the Brussels Effect: one jurisdiction's standards becoming the practical regional standard through commercial logic, without formal agreement.

YOUTH POPULATIONS AND DIGITAL FUTURES

ASEAN's demographic structure creates a governance dimension absent from European debates: the region's extraordinary youth bulge. Median ages across most of Southeast Asia sit below thirty. In the Philippines, it is below twenty-five. These are populations that will spend their entire adult lives interacting with AI systems in ways that current governance frameworks were not designed to address.

The implications for governance priorities are significant. Europe's AI governance debates are shaped by the concerns of mature democracies with established welfare states: privacy, accountability, worker protection and democratic integrity. These concerns are real in Southeast Asia too, but the more urgent question for young populations entering labour markets is different: will AI systems expand or contract opportunity? Will AI-mediated hiring, lending, and educational assessment reproduce existing hierarchies or create new paths for mobility?

Youth-led civil society organisations across ASEAN have begun engaging with these questions in ways that outpace formal governance processes. Digital rights advocates in Indonesia, Thailand, and the Philippines have developed community-led approaches to algorithmic accountability that do not wait for government frameworks. They conduct their own algorithmic audits of platforms that affect young people, publish their findings, and organise collective responses to discriminatory systems.

This bottom-up governance activity is not a substitute for formal regulation. But it represents a form of distributed oversight that formal governance frameworks should be designed to support, not suppress. ASEAN's commitment to consultation and consensus could, in principle, incorporate civil society algorithmic oversight as a recognised governance mechanism. Whether it will is, at present, an open question. For the roughly 300 million Southeast Asians under thirty who will spend their working lives within AI hiring, lending and assessment systems, the answer determines whether algorithmic discrimination compounds across generations or is steadily held in check.

10

DIGITAL COLONIALISM AND TECHNOLOGICAL SOVEREIGNTY

The emails arrived at the inbox of Dr Okuna, a composite figure assembled from documented cases, at the University of Lagos with increasing frequency throughout 2023. Technology companies from Silicon Valley and Shenzhen offered 'partnership opportunities' to deploy their AI systems across Nigerian universities, healthcare facilities, and government agencies. The proposals were generous: free access to cutting-edge AI tools, training for local technicians, and integration support valued at millions of dollars.

But Dr Okuna recognised the pattern. These companies had made similar offers across sub-Saharan Africa, providing sophisticated AI systems developed for Western and Chinese contexts with minimal adaptation for local needs, cultural values, or social structures. The 'partnerships' required exclusive data access agreements, cloud computing dependencies, and technical standards that would make local institutions permanently dependent on external technology providers.[151]

'It's colonialism through code,' Dr Okuna explained to her research team. 'They're offering us advanced technology in exchange for our data, our autonomy, and our ability to develop our own technological capabilities. The AI systems may be sophisticated, but they embed values and assumptions that serve their creators' interests rather than our communities' needs.'

THE NEW SCRAMBLE FOR AFRICA'S DATA

The contemporary rush by technology companies to deploy AI systems across Africa bears an uncomfortable resemblance to the 19th-century colonial Scramble for Africa.[152] Today's scramble focuses on data extraction, market penetration, and technological dependency. Mineral wealth and territorial control were the objectives of the last century; the fundamental dynamics of extraction and exploitation remain unchanged.

Major technology companies from the United States, China, and Europe have established AI research centres, data collection operations, and deployment programmes across Africa with the stated goal of 'bringing advanced technology to underserved populations.' These initiatives often provide genuine benefits: improved healthcare diagnostics, better educational resources and expanded access to digital services. But the terms reveal extractive relationships disguised as development assistance.

Google's AI research centre in Ghana focuses on developing AI applications for African contexts while retaining ownership and control of intellectual property, algorithms, and data-processing capabilities.[153] Local researchers contribute expertise and cultural knowledge, but the fundamental technological capabilities remain under the control of external entities. When these researchers develop innovations, the patents belong to Google. When they identify valuable applications, the profits flow to California.

The extraction goes beyond intellectual property to data sovereignty. African users generating data through Google services do not control how that data is used, where it is stored, or who profits from it. Health data from African patients trains medical AI that African hospitals must pay to access. Agricultural data from African farmers is used to develop precision farming systems that require expensive subscriptions. Educational data from African students creates learning systems that African schools cannot afford.

Chinese technology companies have established similar patterns through Belt and Road Initiative AI projects (the Belt and Road being China's multi-trillion-dollar programme of infrastructure investment and financing across Africa, Asia, and beyond) that provide advanced technology infrastructure while creating dependencies on Chinese technology standards, governance systems, and economic relationships.[154] Huawei's Safe City initiatives across Africa provide AI-powered surveillance and security systems that African governments could not otherwise afford.[155] However, these systems operate through Chinese-controlled infrastructure, use Chinese technical standards, and require Chinese expertise for maintenance. African governments gain capability but lose autonomy.

Dr Abeba Birhane at Trinity College Dublin argues that these patterns constitute 'algorithmic colonialism', in which technological development serves external interests while local communities are on the receiving end.[156] 'African data trains AI systems that primarily benefit wealthy countries, while African communities become dependent on external technology providers they cannot control or modify. We provide the raw materials (data) and buy back the finished products (AI services) at prices we cannot afford. It's digital colonialism with better marketing.'

LANGUAGE IMPERIALISM THROUGH AI

The dominance of English-language AI development creates subtle but pervasive forms of linguistic colonialism that privilege English communication patterns while marginalising the 2,000-plus languages spoken across Africa.

Swahili, spoken by over 100 million Africans, has minimal AI support despite being one of the world's major languages.[157] The limited natural language processing available treats Swahili as simplified English, ignoring its unique grammatical structures, tonal patterns, and cultural embeddings. Swahili's noun class system, which encodes meaning through prefixes indicating size, shape, and animacy, becomes invisible to AI systems that parse language using English grammar.

The linguistic imperialism extends to knowledge representation. African oral traditions, which encode sophisticated historical, ecological, and social knowledge in narrative form, are invisible to AI systems that privilege written documentation. Griots (West African storytellers, poets, musicians, and oral historians) who maintain centuries of genealogical, historical, and cultural information through oral tradition are dismissed as 'lacking data' by AI systems that recognise only written records.

Indigenous click languages like Xhosa and Zulu face even greater marginalisation. Their phonetic structures, tonal variations, and grammatical constructions are so different from English that AI systems cannot process them. Speakers must translate their thoughts into English to interact with AI, thereby losing nuance, meaning, and cultural identity in the process.

ECONOMIC DEPENDENCY AND VALUE EXTRACTION

Digital colonialism operates through economic relationships that create dependency on external technology providers while extracting value from local communities. AI systems offered as 'free' services involve hidden costs through data extraction, market penetration, and technological lock-in. External providers capture the value; local users provide it.

Cloud computing dependencies represent particularly insidious forms of technological colonialism.[158] African institutions that store data and run computations on Amazon Web Services, Microsoft Azure, or Alibaba Cloud become dependent on foreign infrastructure they do not control. Sovereignty evaporates when critical government data resides on servers subject to foreign jurisdiction.

The dependency goes beyond data storage to computational capacity. African institutions lacking local computing infrastructure must pay foreign companies for every AI calculation. Training a medical diagnosis model costs thousands of dollars in cloud computing fees. Running agricultural predictions requires ongoing subscriptions. The promise of AI-enabled development becomes rent extraction by foreign technology companies.

The economic extraction extends to human capital. Africa's best AI researchers are recruited by foreign technology companies, contributing to brain drain that undermines local technological development. The few AI experts who remain often work for the regional offices of foreign companies, developing AI for external markets. Local needs remain unaddressed.

A Kenyan AI researcher working for a Silicon Valley company described the dilemma: 'I'm developing cutting-edge AI, but for American problems. Agricultural AI for industrial farms, not smallholder plots. Medical AI for insured patients, not rural clinics. Financial AI for credit cards, not mobile money. I'm using African talent to solve Western problems while African problems remain unsolved.'

RESISTANCE AND TECHNOLOGICAL SOVEREIGNTY

The picture of digital colonialism would be incomplete without recording that it is contested. African technologists, policymakers, and communities are not passive recipients of externally imposed technology. Across the continent, deliberate efforts to build technological sovereignty are producing results.

The African Continental Free Trade Area (AfCFTA) digital protocol includes provisions for data governance and AI development that prioritise African sovereignty over foreign dependency. Implementation remains incomplete, but the political commitment represents a structural break from previous patterns of accepting technology on terms set by external providers.

Numerous African countries have enacted data protection legislation modelled partly on GDPR but adapted to local contexts. Ethiopia, Nigeria, South Africa, and Kenya have all moved to establish domestic regulatory frameworks for data and AI. These frameworks are imperfect and enforcement capacity is uneven, but they create the legal basis for domestic governance of AI systems that operate within national territory.

The Pan-African Data Governance Framework, under development at the African Union level, seeks to create a continental approach to AI data sovereignty that neither surrenders to foreign standards nor fragments into incompatible national approaches. The negotiations are slow and technically difficult. They are also necessary.

THE MASAKHANE MODEL

The most concrete example of African technological self-determination in AI is Masakhane, a grassroots community of African researchers building natural language processing for African languages. The name comes from the isiZulu phrase 'let us build together': a deliberate rejection of the extractive model in which external actors develop AI using African data and African talent, with benefits flowing outward.

Masakhane's model inverts the colonial pattern. Research capacity stays in Africa. Intellectual property belongs to the community. Development priorities are set by African researchers working on African problems. The results serve African communities first.

By 2024, the initiative had developed NLP tools for over sixty African languages, demonstrating that the technical gap was never about fundamental difficulty but about investment priorities. The languages that Silicon Valley's AI systems cannot handle are not harder to model. They simply generated insufficient commercial return to attract corporate investment. The Masakhane researchers showed that a different investment logic produces different results.

The model has implications beyond language technology. It demonstrates that the technological dependency characterising AI colonialism is not technically necessary. It is a consequence of where development capacity is concentrated, what problems attract investment, and whose interests shape deployment priorities. All three of these factors are subject to deliberate change.

The Kenyan government's AI strategy, published in 2023, explicitly addressed technological sovereignty as a policy objective. It required that AI systems deployed in government services have locally auditable source code, that government AI contracts include provisions for local capacity development, and that sensitive government data be processed within Kenyan jurisdiction. Whether these provisions are enforced with rigour or treated as aspirational language will determine whether they change outcomes. The political will to require them represents a meaningful departure from previous technology procurement practice.

DATA COMMONS AND COLLECTIVE OWNERSHIP

One alternative to both the extractive model of foreign data harvesting and the protectionist model of data localisation is the data commons: a framework for collective ownership and governance of data generated by communities, with benefits flowing to those communities.

The concept draws on the long history of commons governance: of shared resources managed collectively for the benefit of the community, not extracted by private actors. Its application to data requires institutions that most African jurisdictions are still developing: legal frameworks for collective data ownership, technical infrastructure for secure data commons, and governance structures that give communities genuine authority over how their data is used.

Several pilot projects demonstrate the concept's viability. A data commons for agricultural knowledge in East Africa enables smallholder farmers to collectively share crop performance data, weather observations, and market information, with AI systems trained on the commons providing recommendations back to contributing farmers. The value created by the data stays within the farming community; it does not flow to an external platform.

The challenge is scale. Data commons that work for a few thousand farmers may not provide sufficient data diversity to train models that perform well across a broader range of conditions. The scale advantages that make large centralised data repositories attractive to AI developers are real. Finding governance models that capture those advantages without surrendering community control is the technical and institutional challenge that data commons advocates are working to resolve.

11

BUILDING BRIDGES: CROSS-CULTURAL AI DEVELOPMENT

The video conference screen showed researchers from MIT and Stanford alongside colleagues from universities in Lagos, Mumbai, São Paulo, and Jakarta. The project they were discussing had taken three years to organise and represented one of the most ambitious attempts at genuinely cross-cultural AI development: creating a multilingual, multicultural educational AI system that could work across radically different educational contexts without imposing any single cultural framework.

'Our prototypes were disasters,' Dr Chen described. 'We essentially created American educational AI with language translation layers. The Indian team pointed out that our individual achievement focus conflicted with collaborative learning traditions. The Nigerian team showed us how our knowledge validation systems excluded traditional expertise. The Brazilian squad demonstrated that our assessment methods were culturally inappropriate for community-based education.'[159]

The breakthrough came when the team abandoned the idea of creating a universal system and instead developed a platform that could be locally adapted while maintaining interoperability. Each cultural context could implement educational approaches that reflected local values, while still allowing students to collaborate across cultural boundaries when appropriate.

PARTICIPATORY DESIGN ACROSS CULTURES

Cross-cultural AI development requires moving beyond consultation to genuine participatory design, in which different cultural communities are partners in creating technological solutions, not recipients of externally developed systems.

The Global Partnership on AI has pioneered participatory design methodologies that involve multiple cultural communities as co-creators of AI systems.[160] These approaches require extensive development of cultural competency, relationship building, and flexible technical architectures that can accommodate diverse cultural requirements.

The process begins with what the partnership calls 'epistemic humility', recognising that Western approaches to knowledge and intelligence are not universal but culturally specific. Technical teams spend months learning about local knowledge systems, understanding how communities define intelligence, and recognising what problems communities actually want solved versus what outsiders think they need.

In Tanzania, a participatory health AI project began with six months of community engagement before any coding began.[161] Technical teams lived in villages, participated in daily life, and learned how health decisions were made. They discovered that individual health was inseparable from family wellbeing, that traditional healers provided psychological support that hospitals could not, and that health included spiritual dimensions that Western medicine ignored. The resulting AI system facilitated family health conferences rather than providing individual diagnoses. Instead of replacing traditional healers, it provided them with additional information and support.

The Maasai Technology Collaborative in Kenya and Tanzania represents another innovative approach to participatory AI development.[162] Maasai communities partner with international researchers to develop AI systems for traditional pastoral management while maintaining cultural autonomy and traditional governance structures. Maasai elders, not technical experts, defined project goals. Traditional ecological knowledge was treated as equal to scientific data. Community benefit, not technical innovation, is the measure of success.

The resulting system combines satellite imagery with traditional weather prediction, GPS tracking with indigenous cattle management, and analytics with generational wisdom. Pastoralists still read natural signs but receive additional satellite data. They maintain traditional grazing patterns, but with early warning about conflicts or droughts.

Brazilian favela communities have developed their own approach to participatory AI design through community technology centres.[163] Residents learn basic AI skills, identify local problems, and develop solutions with technical support, not external direction. One favela developed a safety AI controlled by residents, with no outside police surveillance imposed. The system identifies dangerous situations and alerts community members, but data remains under community control. Residents decide what constitutes danger, who receives alerts, and how to respond.

TECHNICAL BRIDGES AND CULTURAL AUTONOMY

Cross-cultural AI development requires technical architectures that enable interoperability without imposing uniformity. Systems must communicate across cultural boundaries while maintaining distinct approaches, technical bridges that preserve cultural autonomy.

Federated learning enables communities to collaborate on AI development without sharing raw data.[164] Each community maintains control over their information while contributing to collective capabilities. African health organisations use federated learning to develop diagnostic AI without exposing patient data.[165] Each hospital trains models on local data, sharing only model updates, not patient information. The collective system learns from diverse populations while maintaining data sovereignty.

Modular architectures allow different cultural communities to implement culturally appropriate interfaces while sharing computational infrastructure.[166] An agricultural AI platform developed through collaboration in Southeast Asia demonstrates this modularity.[167] The core system processes satellite imagery, weather data, and soil information. But each country implements culturally specific interfaces. Thai farmers receive guidance aligned with sufficiency economy principles. Vietnamese farmers get collectivist recommendations for cooperative farming. Filipino farmers obtain information in a format suited to *bayanihan* (community cooperation) approaches.

Open-source development enables communities to modify AI systems for local needs while contributing improvements globally.[168] The African Language Technology initiative develops open-source natural language processing for African languages.[169] African developers are not waiting for Google or Microsoft to get around to it; they are creating their own language models. The open-source approach means that every improvement benefits everyone. Collective capability accumulates; competitive advantage is not the point.

SUCCESS METRICS BEYOND EFFICIENCY

Cross-cultural AI evaluation requires measures beyond speed, accuracy, and profit metrics, measures that reflect diverse values and priorities.

Seven-generation thinking Iin North American indigenous traditions evaluates AI's impact on future generations, not on quarterly earnings.[170] A renewable energy AI system developed in collaboration with indigenous communities in Canada evaluates success based on seven-generation impact.[171] Maximising immediate energy production is not the objective; the system optimises for long-term sustainability. Success means the availability of energy for their grandchildren's grandchildren.

Gross National Happiness metrics from Bhutan evaluate AI in terms of well-being, not productivity.[172] Bhutanese educational AI measures success through student happiness, cultural preservation, spiritual development, and academic achievement.[173] The system might recommend fewer study hours if students show stress, suggest traditional activities alongside modern curricula, and prioritise balance over optimisation.

Ubuntu metrics from African philosophy prioritise collective flourishing over individual optimisation.[174] AI succeeds when it strengthens social bonds, not just personal efficiency. South African housing AI, using Ubuntu metrics, allocates resources based on community impact, not individual need alone.[175] Extended families receive priority over individuals. Communities with strong social networks receive investment to preserve cohesion.

Pacific Island resilience metrics evaluate AI on adaptation capacity, not current performance.[176] Kiribati's climate adaptation AI measures success by preserving cultural identity during forced migration, not by economic metrics.[177] The system helps communities maintain language, traditions, and social structures while relocating. GDP might fall, but cultural continuity ensures community survival.

These diverse metrics reveal that success is culturally determined, not technically absolute. AI systems must be evaluated according to what communities value, not what developers measure most easily.

THE LIMITS OF TECHNICAL BRIDGES

Cross-cultural AI development faces genuine limits that should be acknowledged without pretending the problems are simpler than they are.

Power imbalances persist even in well-intentioned collaborative projects. When MIT researchers partner with Lagos universities, the MIT team controls funding, publication, and ultimately deployment decisions. Participation without power is consultation dressed as partnership. True co-creation requires structural reforms that most Western academic institutions find threatening.

Language barriers extend beyond translation. Cultural concepts often have no equivalent in other languages, and forcing them into English-language frameworks distorts their meaning. A Māori concept of collective responsibility cannot be cleanly mapped to Western individualist legal frameworks. An indigenous understanding of the relationship with the land cannot be summarised in an API parameter. Genuine cross-cultural AI development requires operating in multiple conceptual frameworks simultaneously, which is cognitively and technically demanding in ways that convenient translation workarounds cannot resolve.

Time horizons conflict. Silicon Valley operates on eighteen-month product cycles. Indigenous communities think in generations. Research institutions work on three-to-five year grants. Community-centred development takes the time communities require. These incompatibilities are real, and no amount of good intentions makes them disappear.

A Japanese government official described this honestly: 'We have learned that building AI bridges between cultures takes twice as long as building AI for a single market, costs three times as much, and produces something that looks less impressive in a demonstration but actually works. Funders find this difficult.'

The honest conclusion of cross-cultural AI development is not that it is impossible, but that it requires sustained institutional commitments that run counter to how technology development is currently organised and funded. The bridges can be built. They require different foundations than the ones currently on offer.

THE EVALUATION PROBLEM

Cross-cultural AI development ultimately faces a measurement challenge: how do you know if you have succeeded? The standard metrics (accuracy, efficiency and user satisfaction) are not culturally neutral. They measure what developers have decided to measure, using frameworks that may not reflect the values of the communities the systems serve.

A health AI that is highly accurate at predicting individual patient needs but disrupts family consultation processes may be a technical success and a social failure. An agricultural AI that maximises yield but violates cultural protocols around land use has succeeded on the metrics its developers chose while failing on the metrics the community would choose.

Developing evaluation frameworks that reflect community values requires involving communities in defining success before development begins. This is harder than it sounds. Community preferences are not uniform; communities contain internal disagreements about values and priorities. Traditional governance structures may not map cleanly onto the inclusive participation ideals of participatory design methodology. And the process of defining evaluation criteria is itself a technical process that requires communities to engage with concepts (statistical validity, measurement error, fairness metrics) that may not have obvious translations into local frameworks.

Several organisations working in cross-cultural AI development have converged on similar approaches to this challenge. They distinguish between *process legitimacy* and *outcome legitimacy*. Process legitimacy means that the community genuinely participated in designing the system. Outcome legitimacy means that the system produces outcomes that the community considers good. Both are necessary; neither is sufficient.

A system can have process legitimacy (extensive community involvement, genuine co-design) and still produce outcomes that the community later finds inadequate, because the consequences were not fully predictable during design. A system can produce outcomes the community values while having been developed with minimal participation, if the developers happen to guess correctly about community values. In practice, process legitimacy is the more reliable path to outcome legitimacy, because communities that participated in design are better placed to identify problems and demand adjustments when outcomes fall short.

THE INTERMEDIARY GAP

Between the large-scale cross-cultural AI projects described in this chapter and the individual communities affected by AI systems lies an intermediary gap: the scarcity of organisations that can bridge technical expertise and community knowledge in sustained, accountable ways.

Technical experts with genuine cross-cultural competency are rare. Community organisations with sufficient technical knowledge to engage meaningfully in AI design processes are rarer. The organisations that can do both, maintaining genuine technical credibility while sustaining deep accountability to specific communities, are rarer still.

This gap cannot be filled entirely by individual practitioners, however skilled. It requires institutional investment: in training programmes that develop technically capable practitioners with genuine cross-cultural competency, in community organisations that develop the technical literacy to engage on equal terms with AI developers, and in funding models that support sustained engagement rather than project-by-project consultation.

The Digital Stewards model, training community members in technical skills with the explicit goal of building community capability, represents one approach to addressing the institutional gap. Organisations like Masakhane, which build research capacity within communities and do not import external expertise, represent another. Neither model scales automatically; both require sustained support and are chronically underfunded relative to the commercial AI development they are meant to help communities manage.

The good news is that models exist. The work is not starting from scratch. The scaling requires investment decisions by governments, foundations, and development institutions that those actors have not yet made at the required scale. That is a political and institutional problem, not a technical one.

PART III

GOVERNING THE UNGOVERNABLE

WHO CONTROLS THE MACHINE?
THE SHORT ANSWER IS: NOT YOU.

12

THE POLICY PUZZLE: REGULATING INVISIBLE POWER

On the morning of 22 May 2018, Mark Zuckerberg appeared before the European Parliament in Brussels to answer questions about Cambridge Analytica, the political data firm that had harvested Facebook user data to build voter profiles for targeted campaign messaging, and Facebook's data practices.[178] The session was, by most accounts, a procedural disappointment. MEPs asked questions but received answers calibrated for a press release. Zuckerberg thanked each questioner warmly before saying something carefully imprecise. The session ended. European parliamentarians returned to their offices. Facebook's share price recovered.

The encounter crystallised something that regulators across the world were beginning to understand: the tools for governing technology built during the industrial age were poorly suited to governing technology built during the information age. Industrial regulation assumes you can inspect a machine. You can walk through a factory. You can test a product. You can trace a supply chain. With algorithmic systems, the machine is invisible, the product is probabilistic, and the supply chain passes through infrastructure that exists in no particular jurisdiction.

The woman running the EU's digital single market policy at the time, a senior official based in Brussels named Petra, described the institutional challenge: 'We regulate financial products. We regulate pharmaceuticals. We regulate food. We have decades of methodology for those domains. For AI, we had to invent a regulatory theory from nothing, while the technology moved faster than our committee timetable.'[179]

THE VOCABULARY OF AI REGULATION

Before examining specific regulatory frameworks, it helps to have a common vocabulary. The discussion of AI governance proceeds in a language that has not yet been standardised, which creates confusion that is sometimes genuine and sometimes strategically cultivated.

Algorithmic transparency refers to the degree to which an AI system's decision process can be understood and explained. This ranges from full transparency, where the logic is open to public inspection, through partial transparency, where auditors can inspect it under controlled conditions, to opacity, where even the system's developers cannot fully explain a given output. Most commercial AI systems sit somewhere in the partial-to-opaque range.

Accountability asks who is responsible when an AI system causes harm. The answer is more complex than it appears. The data used to train the model came from a single set of organisations. The model itself was built by another. It was integrated into a product by a third. The product was deployed by a fourth. The decision that caused harm was technically made by the algorithm, legally made by the organisation that deployed it, and effectively made by a procurement officer who signed a contract. Distributing responsibility across this chain is a genuine legal challenge that most existing frameworks have yet to resolve.

Auditability refers to the ability to examine an AI system retrospectively to determine what it did and why. Many current systems generate minimal logs. Decisions made by opaque models may be practically irreproducible: the same input may produce a different output if queried at a different time, or after the model has been updated. Regulating something that leaves no reliable record of its own behaviour requires novel approaches.

Sandboxes are controlled regulatory environments where new technologies can be tested before general deployment, with regulators involved in the testing from the start.[180] The Financial Conduct Authority's sandbox model, developed in the UK for fintech, has become influential across AI regulation. Singapore adopted a version; Canada's federal government explored one; the EU's AI Act incorporated a provision for them. The basic idea is sound: regulated experimentation before widespread harm is preferable to widespread harm followed by retrospective intervention. The implementation challenge is determining what constitutes adequate testing and who bears liability during the test period.

THREE REGULATORY PHILOSOPHIES

AI governance approaches globally cluster into three broad philosophies, though most real systems blend elements of each.

Rights-based regulation starts from fundamental rights (privacy, dignity, non-discrimination, due process) and asks whether an AI system respects or violates them. This is the approach most consistent with European legal traditions. It is well-suited to identifying specific harms but less well-suited to managing systemic risks that emerge from the aggregate behaviour of many AI systems, none of which individually violates rights.

Risk-based regulation classifies AI applications by the severity of potential harm and applies proportionate oversight. High-risk applications (criminal justice, healthcare, employment, credit) face more stringent requirements than low-risk applications like spam filters or recommendation algorithms. This is pragmatically sensible but raises questions about who determines risk levels and how classifications adapt as applications evolve.

Innovation-first regulation treats regulation primarily as a facilitative tool, prioritising conditions under which AI development flourishes, with constraints applied only when demonstrated harm requires intervention. This approach characterises most early US federal policy and most East Asian frameworks outside of China. Its advocates argue that premature regulation suppresses beneficial innovation; its critics note that demonstrated harm in a complex technological system may emerge long after the problematic design choices have become deeply embedded.

Heinrich, a member of the Bundestag's digital committee, described the philosophical tension in terms his constituency understood: 'My voters ask me two things. First, they ask why their bank denied their mortgage, and no one can tell them why. Second, they ask why Germany's AI sector continues to lose engineers to San Francisco. Both complaints are legitimate. They pull in exactly opposite directions.'

THE ACCOUNTABILITY GAP IN PRACTICE

The gap between algorithmic decisions and human accountability generates harm at scale. The examples are not hypothetical.

Robert, a welfare recipient in a British city, had his benefits terminated by an automated system without explanation.[181] He appealed. The appeal was reviewed by a worker who had access to the system's output but not its reasoning. The worker upheld the termination. Robert contacted a legal aid organisation. They found that the algorithm had flagged him as a fraud risk because he had changed his address twice in eighteen months. He had moved when his landlord raised the rent. The system had no mechanism for distinguishing legitimate address changes from suspicious behaviour. The benefit termination persisted for four months before a tribunal overturned it. By that point, Robert had accumulated debt from rent arrears and was at risk of eviction.

This is not exceptional. It is routine. It is the logical consequence of deploying systems that generate consequential outputs without adequate explanation mechanisms, and then layering human review processes on top that do not give reviewers sufficient information to exercise genuine judgment.

The legal challenge is formidable. Existing legislation for challenging adverse decisions assumes a decision-maker who can be questioned and whose reasoning can be examined. When the decision-maker is a model trained on historical data using gradient descent, an optimisation process that iteratively adjusts a model's internal settings to minimise its error rate, the question 'why did you decide this?' is genuinely difficult to answer in terms a tribunal can work with.

Some jurisdictions have begun requiring **explainability** as a legal standard. The EU's General Data Protection Regulation includes a right not to be subject to solely automated decisions with significant effects, and a right to explanation when automated decisions are made.[182] The practical implementation of this right remains contested. Does a meaningful explanation require algorithmic transparency? A statement of the factors considered? The ability to contest the specific inputs? Courts in different European jurisdictions have reached different conclusions.

DEMOCRATIC DEFICITS AND INVISIBLE CHOICES

AI systems encode choices about values, priorities, and acceptable tradeoffs. These choices have traditionally been made through democratic or professional processes. When they migrate into algorithmic systems, they become invisible.

A sentencing algorithm does not merely predict recidivism. It encodes a view about how heavily past arrests should be weighted against future likelihood of reoffending. It encodes a view about whether demographic characteristics that correlate with crime are legitimate predictors. It encodes a view about what level of false-positive rate is acceptable when the cost of a false positive is years in prison. These are moral and political questions. They are being answered by software engineers under commercial constraints, without public deliberation.

The democratic deficit is structural. Procurement processes for algorithmic systems rarely require disclosure of the values encoded in the system. The public officials who sign purchasing contracts often lack the technical capacity to evaluate what they are buying. The communities affected by the systems are rarely consulted during design. The feedback loops that normally allow democratic systems to identify and correct errors (journalism, legal challenge, electoral accountability) function poorly when the decision-making is opaque and the harm is distributed across thousands of individual cases.

Katja, a compliance officer at a German local authority, described the practical situation: 'I am responsible for ensuring our procurement complies with data protection law. I am not a software engineer. I read the vendor's documentation. It says the system is compliant with GDPR. It says it is explainable. What I cannot do is verify those claims. I am taking the vendor's word for it. If I am taking the vendor's word for it, what does compliance actually mean?'[183]

This is the accountability gap from the regulator's side: not malice, but a structural mismatch between the complexity of the systems and the capacity of the institutions meant to oversee them.

WHAT ADEQUATE REGULATION LOOKS LIKE

The emerging consensus among researchers who have studied this question across multiple jurisdictions is that adequate AI regulation requires several elements that most current frameworks lack.

Mandatory impact assessments before deployment, not after harm has occurred. Analogous to environmental impact statements, these would require organisations deploying high-risk AI systems to assess and disclose likely effects on affected communities, with an independent review before deployment proceeds.

Algorithmic auditing by independent third parties with genuine access to systems, data, and deployment records, not self-reported compliance documentation. The financial audit model is imperfect but instructive: financial accounts are not self-assessed and self-reported by companies; they are independently verified. There is no obvious reason that AI systems affecting consequential decisions should receive less scrutiny than balance sheets.

Meaningful redress mechanisms that give affected individuals the ability to challenge algorithmic decisions with genuine information and genuine prospects of success. This requires both adequate explanation and accessible legal or administrative processes.

Public sector leadership through procurement standards that require transparency and auditability. Governments collectively constitute enormous markets for AI services. Procurement standards that require genuine explainability, algorithmic auditing, and redress mechanisms would reshape what vendors offer.

None of this is technically impossible. All of it is politically difficult because it requires constraining systems that benefit powerful organisations. The difficulty is not understanding what adequate governance looks like. The difficulty is generating the political will to require it.

Heinrich summarised this without diplomatic softening: 'We know what to do. We are not doing it fast enough.'

13

EUROPE'S AI ACT, TEMPLATE OR CAUTIONARY TALE?

In March 2024, the European Parliament voted to adopt the EU Artificial Intelligence Act: the world's first comprehensive binding legal framework for AI systems.[184] The vote was 523 in favour, 46 against. The Act had taken four years to negotiate, survived multiple drafts, weathered a furious lobbying effort by major AI companies, and was amended substantially after the release of large language models, AI systems trained on vast collections of text and capable of generating fluent prose, answering questions, and performing a wide range of language tasks, made the original draft look inadequate. By the time it passed, it was longer than the Treaty of Rome.

Whether it represents a genuine model for AI governance or a cautionary tale about the limits of regulatory ambition in the face of technological acceleration is a question that will take a decade to answer. For now, it is the most substantive attempt by any jurisdiction to govern AI comprehensively, and it merits serious examination.

WHAT THE ACT DOES

The EU AI Act takes a risk-based approach, classifying AI applications into four tiers according to the severity of potential harm.

Prohibited practices include AI systems that manipulate users through subliminal techniques, exploit vulnerabilities of specific groups (children, people with disabilities), enable governments to conduct social scoring for general purposes, and engage in most real-time remote biometric surveillance in public spaces. These are banned outright.

High-risk applications (criminal justice, employment, credit, education, healthcare, immigration, critical infrastructure) face the most demanding requirements: mandatory conformity assessments, technical documentation, human oversight provisions, transparency with affected persons, and registration in a public database. Operators must implement risk management systems and post-market monitoring.

Limited-risk applications face transparency obligations: users must be told they are interacting with AI in certain contexts, and AI-generated content must be labelled.

Minimal-risk applications (spam filters, recommendation algorithms, most entertainment AI) face no mandatory requirements under the Act, though industry codes of conduct are encouraged.

The Act's enforcement architecture places primary responsibility on member states, which must designate national competent authorities. The European AI Office, established in 2024, coordinates and enforces rules on general-purpose AI models.

Fines for non-compliance are graduated by violation type. Violations involving prohibited practices can attract penalties of up to €35 million or 7% of global annual turnover, whichever is higher.[185] Violations of other obligations attract lower tiers. The 7% fine tier for the most serious violations is the provision that makes general counsel at technology companies reach for antacids.

THE BRUSSELS EFFECT

The EU's approach to regulation has a structural feature that makes it disproportionately influential beyond its own borders: the Brussels Effect, documented by Columbia Law professor Anu Bradford.[186]

The mechanism is straightforward. Companies that operate globally cannot practically maintain different product versions for different regulatory regimes. Compliance with the strictest standard is cheaper than simultaneous compliance with multiple standards. When the EU's market is large enough to matter, and at 450 million consumers it is, the EU's standards become the de facto global standard. European data protection law shaped global data practices well before the GDPR was emulated by other jurisdictions. European consumer product safety standards influenced manufacturing worldwide. European food safety standards reshaped agricultural supply chains.

The same dynamic is now operating on AI. Major AI companies are building systems that comply with the EU AI Act because those systems will also be deployed in Europe, and maintaining separate EU and non-EU versions is operationally unattractive. Regulatory compliance becomes a design constraint at the architecture level, not a bolt-on afterthought.

The Brussels Effect is not sovereignty. It is power through scale, the power to impose your standards on people who do not vote in your elections because they cannot otherwise access your market. It operates through commercial incentives, not diplomatic negotiation, which makes it both more effective and less democratically transparent than formal international agreements.

ISABELLE'S OBJECTION

Isabelle, a French digital rights researcher based in Lyon, has spent years tracking the distance between the AI Act's stated ambitions and its practical provisions.[187]

'The Act was written in a particular historical moment,' she explained. 'The negotiators had in mind narrow AI systems that do specific things: a face recognition system, a credit scoring model. Then GPT-4 arrived, and suddenly, the most consequential AI systems were general-purpose systems that do not fit neatly into any use category. The Act was amended to address this, but the amendments were negotiated under time pressure and have significant gaps.'

Her specific concern was with general-purpose AI models: systems like large language models that can be applied to many purposes, some high-risk and some not, and that are deployed through layers of developers and deployers, not directly by the foundational model provider.

'Who is responsible for a large language model that is used to generate fraudulent financial advice? The company that trained the model? The company that built an application using the model? The user who prompted the output? The Act tries to assign responsibility across the value chain, but the chain is long, and the liability assignment is genuinely contested.'

Her second concern was with enforcement capacity. 'We have created an extremely detailed compliance framework. It requires technical documentation, conformity assessments and risk management systems. Do member states have the technical capacity to evaluate whether those documents describe real systems? In most cases, no. We will have excellent compliance documentation and a limited ability to verify whether it corresponds to the actual system.'

This is not a reason not to regulate. It is a reason to build regulatory capacity: to invest in the technical expertise that national authorities will need to enforce genuinely, not just formally. Whether that investment is occurring at the required scale remains uncertain at this point.

SINGAPORE'S COMPLEMENT

While the EU built a comprehensive legal framework, Singapore developed a complementary principles-based advisory framework combined with targeted sector-specific rules.[188]

The Infocomm Media Development Authority's Model AI Governance Framework, revised in 2020, provides practical guidance for organisations deploying AI, not a binding regulation but detailed, technically informed recommendations for risk assessment, explainability, and human oversight. The framework is explicitly designed to facilitate responsible AI deployment, not to constrain it, reflecting Singapore's economic priorities as a financial and technology hub.

The city-state has invested heavily in regulatory capacity. The Monetary Authority of Singapore has AI specialists embedded in its supervisory teams, capable of assessing the algorithmic systems they oversee. The model is less ambitious in scope than the EU Act but arguably more realistic about the enforcement capacity required to make regulation meaningful. Theatre is not enforcement.

The tension between the EU and Singapore approaches to AI governance illuminates a genuine dilemma in AI governance: comprehensive, binding regulation without adequate enforcement capacity produces compliance theatre, not accountability. Principles-based guidance with genuine technical capacity may produce more actual change. Neither approach has been operating long enough to demonstrate definitive results.

WHAT THE ACT GETS RIGHT

Despite its complications, the EU AI Act establishes several things that most other regulatory frameworks have avoided.

It names prohibited practices. Drawing a line and saying 'this specific application is not permitted in this jurisdiction' is a more substantive act than issuing principles. The prohibition on government social scoring is not just a guideline. It is a ban.

It creates a public database of high-risk AI systems. Transparency about which systems exist and who operates them is a precondition for democratic oversight. You cannot scrutinise what you do not know exists.

It establishes an individual's right to an explanation for high-risk AI decisions. The practical implementation is contested, but the legal right exists, which creates a basis for litigation and judicial development of the standard.

It recognises that AI governance is an ongoing process, establishing institutions and review mechanisms rather than a static text.

These are genuine contributions to the project of governing AI in a way that protects rights and maintains democratic accountability. The cautionary note is not that the Act is misconceived but that it represents the beginning of a governance project, not its completion.

THE IMPLEMENTATION GAP

Regulation on paper and regulation in practice are different things. The EU AI Act establishes requirements; it does not guarantee that those requirements are met, or that affected people know their rights, or that enforcement authorities have the capacity and will to act when violations occur.

The implementation gap in AI regulation has several dimensions. The most fundamental is technical capacity within national enforcement bodies. The Act assigns primary enforcement responsibility to member states. As of 2024, most EU member states lacked dedicated AI regulatory authorities with genuine technical expertise. Several were in the process of establishing them; others had assigned AI oversight to existing data protection or competition authorities with limited AI-specific capability.

Technical capacity is not purely a budget question. It requires specific skills (machine learning expertise, statistical auditing capability and knowledge of AI system architectures) that are in short supply and in high demand among commercial employers. Regulatory bodies compete for technical talent against companies with substantially larger compensation packages. The result is a chronic gap between the technical demands of AI oversight and the technical capacity of the institutions responsible for it.

The second dimension is awareness. Rights are meaningless if those who hold them do not know they exist. The EU AI Act's rights to explanation for high-risk AI decisions and not to be subject to purely automated decisions with significant effects are not self-executing. They require affected individuals to understand that they have these rights, know how to assert them, and have access to dispute-resolution mechanisms when those rights are violated. None of this is guaranteed by the Act's text alone.

Consumer organisations, civil society groups, and legal aid organisations across Europe are working to build the awareness and access infrastructure that makes the Act's rights real for people who encounter algorithmic decisions in their daily lives. This is necessary and underfunded work. Its results will be a better measure of the Act's actual impact than the elegance of its legal framework.

14

THE BRUSSELS EFFECT MEETS SHENZHEN SPEED

China's approach to AI regulation is itself a study in contrasts with the European model. Shenzhen's AI Industry Promotion Regulation moved from the first public draft to passage in approximately fourteen months, entering force in November 2022 as China's first city-level AI legislation.[189] The comparison with the EU AI Act's four-year negotiation is arithmetically stark and substantively misleading in ways that illuminate the real tension between different governance philosophies.

Shenzhen's speed is possible because the governance framework was drafted by technical specialists within a single-party system, without legislative debate, stakeholder consultation, or the need to reconcile the interests of 27 member states. It is possible because enforcement is handled by a state apparatus that does not face the kind of legal challenge that democratic regulatory decisions routinely attract. It is possible because the framework's primary objective is to facilitate development. Protecting rights is not on the same priority level.

These are not trivial differences. Speed purchased by eliminating accountability mechanisms is not obviously a model to emulate.

CHINA'S NATIONAL AI GOVERNANCE ARCHITECTURE

China has moved faster than any other major power to develop binding AI-specific regulation, though its architecture reflects priorities that differ from European frameworks.[190]

The Provisions on the Management of Algorithmic Recommendations (2022), the Provisions on the Management of Deep Synthesis Internet Information Services (2022, governing synthetic media and deepfakes), and the Interim Measures for the Management of Generative AI Services (2023) constitute a comprehensive, if rapidly developing, national AI governance structure. The speed of China's regulatory development reflects both genuine institutional priority and the administrative advantages of an authoritarian system.

The content of these regulations is notable. They require algorithmic transparency for recommendation systems (users must be able to opt out and understand that they are using recommendation algorithms). They require the labelling of deepfake content. They require AI-generated content to comply with Chinese law, which includes requirements regarding the portrayal of Chinese history and values in approved ways. They require a cybersecurity review of AI systems with significant public influence.

This last requirement functions as a powerful tool for directing AI development toward politically safe applications. It also creates barriers to foreign AI systems operating in China, serving as both a sovereignty assertion and a market protection mechanism.

The governance architecture is real and detailed. Its coherence comes partly from the fact that it does not need to reconcile competing values regarding privacy, free expression, and democratic accountability as European frameworks do. This makes it internally consistent in ways that the EU's framework is not, and it makes it poorly suited as a model for jurisdictions that do hold those values.

THE TECHNOLOGY RACE FRAMING

A significant obstacle to adequate international AI governance is the technology race narrative: the framing of AI development as a geopolitical competition in which regulatory constraints are handicaps that disadvantage nations that impose them relative to rivals that do not.

This framing is promoted aggressively by AI companies because regulatory constraints increase compliance costs and limit certain applications. It resonates with policymakers because technological capability is genuinely linked to economic and military power, and the race framing activates threat-response instincts.

It is also, in important respects, misleading.

First, it conflates AI capability with AI deployment. A jurisdiction that develops capable AI but deploys it responsibly is not falling behind a jurisdiction that deploys the same capability recklessly. A financial system that makes accurate decisions has more value than one that makes faster, inaccurate decisions.

Second, it assumes that the competitive landscape is zero-sum, when the development of international governance standards could create conditions in which all parties benefit from more trustworthy AI systems. The analogy is to financial regulation after 2008: coordinated global standards for financial institutions were not a competitive handicap but a precondition for a functioning financial system.

Third, it obscures the fact that the most consequential competitive advantage in AI is probably not speed of deployment but quality of the underlying systems, which depends on data diversity, research talent, and the kind of collaborative development that is harder to sustain under geopolitical competition.

The technology race framing deserves scrutiny. The policy prescriptions that follow from it (limit regulation, accelerate deployment, treat governance as a cost) are highly convenient for a particular set of commercial interests.

THOMAS'S CALCULATION

Thomas, a Berlin-based startup founder working in industrial AI, explained the Brussels Effect's business logic from the company's perspective.[191]

'We build for European markets. We will comply with the EU AI Act. That is not a choice. So the question is not whether to comply but how, and the follow-on question is whether building compliant systems creates competitive advantage or just costs.

'My view is it creates an advantage. Large industrial clients in Germany, France and Italy are not buying systems that might create legal liability. They will pay a premium for certified, compliant AI because procurement officers do not want to explain to their board why they bought something that turned out to violate the Act. Compliance is a market signal.

'The challenge is that compliance is expensive and the evidence base for what counts as genuinely compliant is still developing. The guidance documents are helpful but not specific enough. We spend substantial time in legal interpretation that would be better spent on engineering.'

This is the business case for regulatory clarity: not that regulation is costless but that clear regulation is preferable to unclear regulation, because uncertainty is itself a cost. Organisations that know exactly what is required can design for compliance. Organisations that do not know what will eventually be required must design defensively across a range of possibilities, which is more expensive and produces worse outcomes.

INTERNATIONAL COORDINATION AND ITS LIMITS

The Global Partnership on AI brings together thirty-plus governments to discuss AI governance principles. The OECD has published AI Principles that have been endorsed by sixty-odd countries. The G7 has issued AI governance commitments. The United Nations has established an AI advisory body. The International Organisation for Standardisation is developing AI standards.

There is no shortage of international governance bodies and principles. There is a shortage of binding international commitments, enforcement mechanisms, and institutional capacity to implement coordination in practice.

The structural obstacle is that binding international agreements require national legislatures to cede some regulatory autonomy, a politically costly step. In a period of rising nationalism and economic competition, the appetite for international regulatory coordination is lower than the problem requires. Countries are simultaneously complaining that AI is ungovernable globally and refusing to agree to the governance structures that would make it governable.

Dr Petrov, a governance researcher at a European research institute, described this as 'the collective action problem at its most classical form: each country prefers that governance norms be established and someone else bear the cost of establishing them.'[192]

The most realistic path to effective international coordination may run through the Brussels Effect, bypassing formal treaty negotiation. If compliance with European standards becomes the de facto global standard through commercial logic, the political problem of securing sovereign states' agreement to binding commitments is bypassed. The democratic legitimacy problem, standards being set by one jurisdiction for everyone, remains. It is a second-best outcome to genuine multilateral coordination. It is more likely to occur.

The Chinese and European regulatory systems will continue to diverge, and the world will inhabit both. That means AI systems designed to operate globally will increasingly have to satisfy requirements from both regulatory regimes, some of which are in tension. How companies and governments handle that tension over the coming decade will substantially determine whether the international governance landscape becomes more or less coherent.

The urgency of this work is considerable. AI systems are being deployed now, in healthcare, criminal justice, employment, and financial services, at a scale that makes 'wait for international consensus' an insufficient response. The harms from inadequate governance accumulate in real lives. Getting governance right is not primarily an abstract policy problem. It is a question of whether the people most affected by algorithmic decisions have any meaningful recourse when those decisions are wrong.

15

DEMOCRATIC DEFICITS IN ALGORITHMIC GOVERNANCE

The neighbourhood was called Bridgeport, and the algorithm was called KERA: the Kinetic Equity Resource Allocator, a name that contained within it all the optimism and avoidance of the era. KERA had been deployed by the city to allocate housing support services across 243 neighbourhoods. It used 17 inputs (including historical service uptake, demographic data, infrastructure condition scores, and a 'resilience index' that no one in the housing department could fully define) to produce quarterly resource allocations.

Lisa had been running a community organisation in Bridgeport for eleven years.[193] She noticed the allocations getting smaller in real terms about eighteen months after KERA was deployed, even as housing need in her neighbourhood visibly increased. She tried to get information about the allocation methodology. The city's response explained that the system was proprietary and that disclosing the methodology might compromise its integrity.

'Proprietary,' she said to us. 'Our neighbourhood's share of public resources is determined by a proprietary algorithm. I am not allowed to know how it works. I am supposed to trust that it is working correctly. On what basis do I trust this?'

She contacted Susan Park, a data journalist who had been investigating algorithmic governance across midwestern cities.[194] Susan's analysis found that KERA allocated consistently smaller shares to neighbourhoods with higher proportions of renters, lower home values, and higher percentages of Black residents, not because of explicit demographic inputs, but because the 'resilience index' used historical service uptake data that reflected decades of prior underinvestment in exactly those neighbourhoods. The algorithm was learning from the pattern it was meant to correct.

THE ALGORITHMIC AUTHORITY TRANSFER

Something significant happens when democratic governance functions are delegated to algorithmic systems: authority is transferred without accountability.

When a city council allocates resources through a committee process, that process is technically open to scrutiny. Meeting minutes are public. Councillors face re-election. Affected communities can attend meetings, present data, and challenge allocations through formal and informal political processes. These mechanisms are imperfect (access is unequal, technical knowledge is unevenly distributed, political processes can be captured by organised interests) but they exist.

When allocation is performed by an algorithm, the transparency mechanisms do not automatically migrate. Proprietary protection may shield the methodology from scrutiny. Technical opacity makes the challenge difficult even when access is granted. Procurement decisions, which are made by officials and not publicised, determine the values encoded in the system long before deployment. By the time the algorithm is running and producing outcomes, the key decisions have already been made in contexts with minimal public oversight.

This is not a consequence of malicious intent. It is a consequence of how technology procurement works in public organisations that lack technical capacity, combined with an inadequate legal framework that does not require algorithmic transparency as a condition for public-sector deployment.

WHO GOVERNS THE GOVERNOR

The governance gap runs in two directions simultaneously.

The first is downward: algorithms making decisions that affect individual people without adequate recourse mechanisms. Lisa's experience with KERA is representative of this direction. The people most affected by algorithmic decisions (recipients of welfare, housing support, healthcare, and criminal justice) are least likely to have the technical knowledge, legal resources, and political access needed to challenge those decisions.

The second is upward: the organisations building and deploying AI systems are inadequately governed by the political and regulatory structures notionally responsible for them. Technology companies routinely access more information about citizens than those citizens have consented to provide, deploy systems with significant social consequences without democratic authorisation, and operate largely outside the accountability structures that govern other powerful institutions.

Jerome, a community organiser in Detroit who had spent three years working on algorithmic accountability in the city's benefit systems, described the governance gap in terms of reversibility.[195] 'When a human caseworker makes a wrong decision, you can appeal. You can get a supervisor. You can get a lawyer. There is a chain of human beings who can say "we were wrong" and change course. When a system makes a wrong decision, and the decision is scaled to 80,000 people, who says "we were wrong"? The vendor has no liability. The city says the vendor is responsible. The vendor's contract indemnifies them. The people who received the wrong decision cannot afford to sue. Nothing changes.'

THE PARTICIPATION PARADOX

Democratic theories of legitimate governance generally require that those affected by decisions have meaningful input into them. AI governance creates what might be called the participation paradox: the decisions most consequential for affected communities are made at the design stage, before deployment, when affected communities have no knowledge that decisions are being made; and the point at which communities can most easily participate, after deployment, is the point at which the most significant choices are already locked in.

A housing support algorithm has, by the time it is deployed, embedded decisions about what counts as need, how historical data should be weighted, what trade-offs between different kinds of accuracy are acceptable, and which errors the system is optimised to avoid. These are value judgements. They are also, in most cases, made by teams of software engineers responding to organisational requirements, not by the communities that will be affected.

Retrospective participation, community consultation after deployment, can surface problems and occasionally lead to modifications. It cannot substitute for participatory design at the point where values are actually encoded. This creates a structural disadvantage for communities without the technical knowledge and institutional access to engage at the design stage, which means that, consistently, the communities are most likely to be harmed by algorithmic systems.

Dr Elena Rodriguez, a political scientist who has studied participatory governance in algorithmic contexts, noted the resulting erosion of a basic democratic norm: 'In democratic theory, the affected community has standing. Their interests matter because they vote, because their consent is required, and because their interests are intrinsically worth considering. Algorithmic governance has found a mechanism to make consequential decisions affecting those communities while effectively removing them from the process. This is not merely a technical problem. It is a democratic problem.'[196]

REBUILDING ACCOUNTABILITY STRUCTURES

Repairing algorithmic accountability does not require abandoning algorithmic systems. It requires ensuring that the accountability structures that apply to consequential public decisions apply to algorithmic decisions as well.

The starting requirement is transparency: public sector algorithmic systems affecting individuals must be documented, and that documentation must be publicly accessible. Not commercially sensitive engineering specifications, but sufficient information to understand what inputs are used, what they are intended to measure, and how the outputs relate to the decisions they inform. Susan Park's analysis of KERA was possible because she obtained limited documentation through a freedom of information request, after a long delay. It should be possible without a three-month legal process.

The second requirement is independent audit. The same organisations that assess algorithmic systems should not be the organisations operating them. Independent technical audit (with genuine access, real enforcement consequences, and public reporting) is the governance mechanism that closes the gap between claimed compliance and actual performance. This exists for financial statements. It does not yet exist, at any consistent scale, for algorithmic public services.

The third requirement is meaningful redress. A legal right to explanation is insufficient if the explanation is incomprehensible or if the redress mechanism is inaccessible. Genuinely accessible challenge mechanisms (accessible in terms of cost, comprehensibility, and realistic prospect of success) are a precondition for algorithmic accountability that is more than notional.

Lisa and Susan's investigation eventually produced a city council review of KERA's allocation methodology. The review resulted in modifications to the resilience index weighting. Bridgeport's allocations increased. The process took two years and required a data journalist, a community organiser, a council member with technical interest, and a sustained campaign.

The fact that the process worked, eventually, is some comfort. The fact that it required all of those elements, and still took two years, tells you rather precisely how adequate the current accountability infrastructure is.

THE PROCUREMENT DECISION

The governance gap in algorithmic systems often begins long before deployment, at the procurement stage where public sector organisations choose what systems to buy and on what terms.

Procurement decisions typically involve a small number of people (procurement officers, technology specialists, senior managers) working within tight time and resource constraints. These decisions establish what systems will be used, on what data, to make what kinds of decisions, with what audit trail, and on what contractual terms. By the time a system is deployed and affecting people's lives, the key governance decisions (about transparency, explainability, bias testing, redress mechanisms) have already been made, typically without any community input.

The asymmetry of information at procurement is severe. Vendors have detailed knowledge of their systems' capabilities and limitations. Procurement officers rarely have equivalent technical knowledge. Vendors have strong commercial incentives to present their systems favourably and limited legal obligations to disclose failure modes, demographic performance disparities, or the values encoded in the system's objective function.

Several jurisdictions have begun requiring algorithmic impact assessments as a condition of public sector procurement. The assessments require procuring organisations to evaluate likely harms before deployment. Investigating them after harm has occurred is the pattern these assessments are meant to break. They vary widely in rigour: some require substantive independent assessment with public reporting; others require self-assessment using checklists. The former is more effective and considerably more expensive. Both are more effective than no assessment at all.

The New York City Local Law 144, requiring bias audits of AI hiring tools, and similar ordinances in several European cities, demonstrate that binding procurement-stage requirements are politically achievable. Scaling these requirements to the full range of public sector AI procurement (welfare, housing, education, criminal justice) is the governance priority that would make the most difference to the largest number of people affected by algorithmic decisions.

Lisa's experience with KERA, and Robert's with the benefits termination algorithm, both began with procurement decisions made years earlier by people who are no longer in their posts, under contracts that did not require the systems to be auditable or explainable or accountable to the people they would affect. Changing those procurement decisions would not have required knowing in advance how the systems would fail. It would have required asking, at the point of procurement, the questions that good governance always requires: who will be affected, how will we know if something goes wrong, and what will we do if it does?

16

PARTICIPATORY DESIGN AND THE LIMITS OF CONSULTATION

Jennifer Liu had been asked to attend the community workshop as a 'stakeholder representative'.[197] The workshop was being run by the city's technology office to gather input on a proposed predictive analytics system for social services allocation. Jennifer was there because she lived in the affected neighbourhood. She was not there because she had been asked what she thought the question was, whether the system was the right tool, or whether the problem it claimed to solve was the problem her community actually experienced.

There were forty people in the room. Twelve were city employees. Eight were consultants from the technology vendor. Four were representatives from advocacy organisations. The remaining sixteen were community members, like Jennifer. They were given thirty minutes for 'input' after a ninety-minute presentation about the system's design and capabilities.

'They explained what the algorithm did,' Jennifer told us afterwards. 'They asked if we had questions. We asked questions. They answered some of them. Then they thanked us for our input and told us the system would launch in the spring. I do not know what they did with our input. I do not know whether it changed anything. I was a box that got ticked.'[198]

This is not a particularly cynical account. It is the standard description of public participation in technology deployment across dozens of municipalities, told by the people on the receiving end of the process.

THE SPECTRUM OF PARTICIPATION

Participation in design exists on a spectrum, and most of what is called participatory design sits closer to one end than the other.

At the minimal end is **information provision**: telling communities about systems that have already been designed, framed as consultation. This is the checkbox-ticking exercise Jennifer describes. It requires no adjustment to the system and provides no genuine influence over outcomes.

Consultation means soliciting feedback on designs that have been substantially settled, with some limited capacity to modify at the margins. Communities are invited to comment. Some comments are incorporated. The fundamental design choices have already been made.

Collaboration involves communities as active participants in design processes, with genuine capacity to influence methodology, data selection, objective function, and error trade-offs. This requires sustained engagement over the design period, not a single workshop.

Co-design treats community members as equal partners in the design process, with shared authority over key decisions. The community is not a source of data or a validation target but an active decision-maker.

Most of what is called 'community engagement' in algorithmic system deployment operates at the information provision or consultation level. The terminology of participation is deployed to satisfy accountability requirements without the substantive transfer of influence that genuine participation would entail.

WHY GENUINE CO-DESIGN IS RARE

The gap between the rhetoric of participation and its practice is not accidental. Genuine co-design is difficult, slow, and threatening to organisational control.

Technical teams have invested months or years in designing systems. Substantial community participation at late design stages means revisiting decisions already made, which creates friction and delay. Project timelines do not accommodate the iterative, relationship-based process that genuine participation requires.

Community members often lack the technical vocabulary to participate effectively in design discussions. Bridging this gap requires investment in community technical capacity (training, accessible documentation, time for learning) that is rarely budgeted for.

Power differentials make genuine participation structurally difficult. Community members participating in consultation with government or corporate bodies are operating in contexts where the other party has vastly more information, institutional authority, and resources. The conditions for genuine equality of input rarely exist.

Ana, who works at a Los Angeles digital rights organisation, described the institutional logic: 'Agencies need to say they consulted the community. Consultation takes one workshop. Genuine co-design takes eighteen months and requires them to cede control over design decisions. No procurement timeline accommodates that. No manager wants to explain to their director that the project is delayed because the community changed the methodology. So you do one workshop.'[199]

WHAT GENUINE PARTICIPATION REQUIRES

The participatory design literature is clear about what moves consultation toward genuine co-design: early involvement, sustained engagement, meaningful decision authority, and community capacity support.

Early involvement means engaging communities before core design choices are made: before the decision that an algorithm is the right tool, before the choice of what data to use, before the definition of the objective. Involving communities after these choices have been made limits participation to adjusting implementation details.

Sustained engagement means ongoing relationships, not single events. Community understanding of technical systems develops through repeated engagement. Relationship-based processes allow trust to develop that makes genuine collaboration possible. One workshop produces consultation theatre.

Meaningful decision authority means that community input must have real consequences. This requires establishing in advance which decisions are subject to community veto or co-determination, and mechanisms for documenting how community input was incorporated or, when it was not incorporated, why.

Community capacity support means investing in the technical literacy that makes genuine participation possible. This includes accessible technical documentation, training in data literacy and algorithmic concepts, and support for community-led technical assessment. It is expensive and it is necessary.

The Detroit Digital Stewards model developed by Allied Media Projects demonstrates what sustained community capacity-building can produce.[200] Participants develop skills in network engineering, data literacy, and algorithmic accountability over an extended training programme. They return to their communities with genuine technical capacity. The result is a community base capable of engaging technical processes from a position of substantive knowledge, not dependent reception.

NAOMI'S QUESTION

Naomi was a software engineer at a mid-sized AI company working on a healthcare appointment scheduling system.[201] She had raised concerns internally about the system's impact on patients with limited English proficiency, who were being allocated longer wait times as a matter of pattern because their communication patterns in the appointment booking system registered as 'high-friction' in the efficiency algorithm.

The company's response had been to add a 'language support flag' that could be set manually by operators. Naomi's concern was that this addressed the symptom without changing the underlying design: the system still optimised for efficiency in ways that disadvantaged the same group.

'We did user testing,' she told us. 'We tested with health professionals, with hospital administrators, with English-speaking patients. Nobody in the testing group experienced the problem that limited-English speakers experience. We never asked: who is not in this room? Who needs to be here for this test to be valid?'

Her question (who is not in this room?) is the practical entry point for participatory design in technology teams that lack diversity and whose testing protocols do not include the people most likely to be harmed.

The fuller version of her question applies to the entire design process. Who was not in the room when we decided what problem to solve? Who was not in the room when we chose the data? Who was not in the room when we decided what accuracy trade-offs to make? Who was not in the room when we defined what counts as success?

In almost every case, the people not in the room are the people who will most directly experience the consequences of the decisions being made.

THE KNOWLEDGE PRODUCTION PROBLEM

Meaningful participation in AI design requires that community members can engage substantively with the design questions being decided. This requires more than goodwill from developers; it requires genuine investment in community technical capacity. And it requires rethinking who is recognised as a knowledge producer in the AI development process.

Standard AI development treats technical expertise as the primary form of relevant knowledge. Data scientists understand the data. Machine learning engineers understand the models. Product managers understand the requirements. Community members understand their 'needs': a category that positions them as consumers of solutions, not producers of knowledge about the problems those solutions are meant to address.

This framing is wrong in a specific way that participatory design literature has documented extensively: the people who will be most affected by a system typically possess the most relevant knowledge about what the system should do, what its failure modes look like, and how it will interact with the social context in which it operates. A welfare recipient knows more about the practical experience of welfare administration than a software engineer. A patient knows more about how a health service actually functions in their community than a product manager who has never been a patient.

Participatory design approaches that genuinely recognise community members as knowledge producers treat their contributions differently from those that merely consult them. They create processes for capturing and integrating community knowledge throughout the design cycle, not only at designated consultation points. They create roles for community members that carry decision authority, not merely advisory status. They compensate community members for their expertise on the same basis as other experts.

THE ACCOUNTABILITY LIFECYCLE

Even well-designed participatory processes face a specific failure mode: the accountability gap after deployment. Communities that participated in design can find themselves with no meaningful mechanism to influence systems that are not performing as expected, or that are producing new harms that were not anticipated during design.

Post-deployment accountability requires mechanisms distinct from those used in design. It requires ongoing monitoring of system performance from a community perspective, accessible channels for raising concerns, responsive processes for addressing those concerns, and, above all, genuine authority to require changes, not merely advise them.

Very few AI deployments include these mechanisms. Pilot programmes that involve communities in design often do not include communities in governance after deployment. The system goes live; the participatory process is declared a success; the community is no longer in the room where decisions are made.

Closing this lifecycle gap requires treating participation not as a design-phase activity but as an ongoing governance commitment. Communities that contributed to design should have representation in the governance bodies that oversee deployed systems. Performance monitoring should include community-defined metrics alongside technical metrics. Complaints from affected individuals should feed into systematic review processes, not be handled as isolated customer service issues.

The municipal level is where these mechanisms are most practically developed. Several US cities, and a growing number of European municipalities, have established algorithmic accountability ordinances that require ongoing community oversight of deployed systems. These ordinances are imperfect: enforcement capacity is often limited, technical capacity in oversight bodies is often thin, and the mechanisms for translating community concerns into system changes are often unclear. They are also the most concrete existing infrastructure for post-deployment community governance of AI systems.

Naomi's question (who is not in this room?) deserves to be asked not only during design, but throughout the life of every AI system that makes consequential decisions about people's lives. The answer will change as the system changes. The question remains the same.

17

ADAPTIVE GOVERNANCE FOR ADAPTIVE SYSTEMS

In 2016, a group of AI researchers coined the term 'concept drift' to describe a specific technical problem: when the real-world distribution of data that a model encounters changes over time, diverging from the distribution on which it was trained, the model's performance degrades.[202] A credit model trained on pre-pandemic data encounters a post-pandemic world where the relationship between employment history and creditworthiness has shifted. A medical diagnostic model trained on pre-vaccine data encounters post-vaccine disease presentations that do not match its training distribution. The world changes. The model does not. Performance declines.

The governance parallel is precise. AI governance frameworks designed for the technological landscape of 2020 encounter the 2026 landscape and exhibit their own form of concept drift. The categories, risk classifications, accountability mechanisms, and enforcement tools that made sense when the frameworks were drafted have not automatically updated to match the systems they are meant to govern.

The challenge for AI governance is to develop adaptive capacity:

frameworks that can evolve as rapidly as the technology without sacrificing the stability and predictability that governance requires.

THE SPEED PROBLEM

The speed differential between technology development and regulatory processes is structural and requires structural solutions.

Technology companies typically operate on development cycles measured in months. Regulatory processes in democratic societies involve consultation, legislative drafting, legal challenge, and implementation phases that typically run in years. The EU AI Act took four years. By the time it passed, the largest AI models had been released, fundamentally changing the landscape the Act was designed to address, and the Act required substantial last-minute amendments.

This is not a failure of the regulatory process. It is a feature of democratic governance: taking time to gather input, build consensus, and anticipate consequences is valuable. But it means that static legislation is chronically behind the technological frontier.

Several adaptive governance mechanisms have been proposed and, in some cases, implemented.

Outcomes-based regulation specifies what systems must achieve rather than how they must be built, creating space for technical approaches to evolve while maintaining stable performance standards. Financial regulation's approach to systemic risk is partly outcomes-based: banks must maintain capital ratios, and how they manage their portfolio to maintain those ratios is their business. The equivalent for AI might be: healthcare diagnostic AI must achieve parity in diagnostic accuracy across demographic groups, without specifying the technical mechanism for achieving that parity.

Adaptive codes of practice allow regulatory expectations to evolve through administrative processes more quickly than through primary legislation. The EU AI Act includes provisions for codes of practice, developed by industry with regulatory input, that can specify technical standards in more detail and be updated more frequently than the Act itself.

Regulatory horizon scanning invests in institutional capacity to identify emerging risks before they become established harms. The UK's Centre for Long-Term Resilience has argued for embedding horizon scanning into the AI regulatory structure, not predicting the future but maintaining ongoing assessment of where new AI capabilities are creating new risk profiles.[203]

Living compliance frameworks build review and update requirements into regulatory instruments from the start. The problem with legislation that becomes outdated is not inherent to legislation; it is a design choice. Regulation that includes mandatory review cycles (every two years, every five years) forces ongoing assessment. The initial framework is not treated as settled.

JIANG WEI AND THE REGULATORY LEARNING PROBLEM

Jiang Wei had been working in China's internet regulatory system for a decade when the generative AI wave arrived.[204] He described the regulatory learning problem in terms that regulators everywhere recognise.

'Our existing framework for internet information services was built for a world of human-created content. Someone writes an article. Someone uploads a video. We have rules for that. We have enforcement mechanisms.

'Generative AI produces content at machine scale. A single model can produce millions of text outputs per day. Our audit processes were not designed for this. We cannot review individual outputs. We can only regulate at the system level, which requires understanding how systems work, which requires the technical capacity we had to build from nothing while the systems were already deployed.'

This is the regulatory learning problem in its acute form: not just that legislation is behind the technology, but that regulatory institutions lack the expertise to understand what they are regulating. Building that expertise takes years. The technology does not wait.

Mika, a Finnish official who had led her country's contribution to the EU AI Act negotiations, described the European institutional response.[205] 'We embedded technical specialists in the negotiating team. We required a technical assessment alongside a legal assessment. We built in provisions for the European AI Office to maintain technical expertise and update guidance. We also made peace with the fact that the Act we passed is not the Act we will need in five years. We have created a framework and institutions. We did not create a permanent solution.'

This realistic assessment (creating framework and institutions, acknowledging these are not permanent solutions) is more honest than most regulatory communications and more useful as a policy stance. Adaptive governance requires accepting that governance will always be a catch-up process and designing institutions accordingly.

THE INDIGENOUS GOVERNANCE CONTRIBUTION

Adaptive governance frameworks from indigenous traditions offer something that Western regulatory theory has consistently undervalued: experience governing complex, dynamic systems over very long time periods.

Traditional Pacific Island navigation systems governed decisions about when to sail, which routes to take, and how to respond to unexpected conditions through distributed decision-making systems that combined accumulated knowledge with real-time environmental reading.[206] These systems were adaptive by design: they encoded historical knowledge but built in mechanisms for responding to novel conditions.

Certain Aboriginal and Torres Strait Islander governance traditions in Australia manage relationships with Country through decision-making frameworks that distinguish between decisions that can be made by present generations and those that require consultation with the accumulated knowledge embodied in elders and cultural law.[207] This multi-temporal decision structure (some decisions made quickly, others requiring longer processes involving deeper legitimacy) offers a model for AI governance that Western administrative frameworks have not replicated.

The Haudenosaunee Confederacy's governance principles, which influenced early thinking about democratic systems in North America, built in mechanisms for evaluating the long-term consequences of decisions that current fast-moving AI regulatory processes largely lack.[208] The principle that present decisions should be evaluated against their consequences for those not yet born is not mysticism; it is a governance methodology that has kept functioning social systems stable across multiple centuries.

These traditions do not map directly onto the challenges of regulating large language models. But they demonstrate that governance frameworks can be designed with adaptive capacity and long-term orientation. The failures of current AI governance (reactive when it should be anticipatory, short-term when it should be multigenerational, static when it should be adaptive) are design failures, not inevitable features of governance.

TOWARD ADAPTIVE INFRASTRUCTURE

The shift from static regulation to adaptive governance requires investment in four forms of infrastructure.

Technical capacity within regulatory bodies. Regulation is only as effective as the regulators' ability to understand what they are regulating. This requires hiring AI specialists for regulatory roles, building technical assessment capabilities, and maintaining ongoing engagement with independent research.

Research and evidence infrastructure. Adaptive governance requires knowing what is happening. This means mandatory incident reporting for AI system failures, independent monitoring of algorithmic decisions in high-stakes domains, longitudinal research on the social consequences of AI deployment, and open-access data about AI system performance in real-world conditions.

International coordination mechanisms. AI systems do not respect borders. Adaptive national governance operating in isolation is insufficient. Coordination mechanisms that enable regulatory learning to be shared across jurisdictions, create common standards where interoperability matters, and address collective action problems in international AI governance are necessary components of an adequate governance infrastructure.

Democratic participation infrastructure. Adaptive governance requires that affected communities have ongoing input into governance processes, not just one-time consultation. This requires investment in digital literacy, accessible participation mechanisms, and institutional structures that give community voices genuine authority.

None of this can be created quickly. All of it can be started immediately. The organisations, institutions, and political will required to begin exist. What is less certain is whether the sense of urgency is sufficient to generate the investment.

The technology will continue to develop regardless of whether governance keeps pace. The question is whether the people affected by it (the people whose benefits are denied, whose credit is rejected, whose faces are misidentified, whose neighbourhoods are under-resourced, whose languages are incomprehensible to the machines making decisions about them) will have adequate recourse. That question is answered by governance, not by technology. It is answered by political choices about whether accountability is a precondition for deployment or an afterthought.

AFTERWORD: THE MIRROR'S EDGE

The problem with mirrors is that they are entirely faithful. They show you exactly what is there.

The problem with AI mirrors is that they show you what was there (the historical record, encoded in training data, reproduced in outputs) and present it as what is. The distinction matters enormously. Facial recognition systems trained on predominantly lighter-skinned faces perform worse on darker faces, not because they have been programmed with prejudice but because they have been trained on a world that already contains prejudice, and they learned from it. Credit models that disadvantage certain postcodes are not inventing discrimination; they are identifying patterns of historical disinvestment and projecting them forward. Recidivism algorithms that correlate with race are not introducing racism into the criminal justice system; they are finding the correlations that systemic racism has already produced in the data and treating them as predictive variables.

The mirror reflects. The problem is what the mirror was pointed at.

This would be a tractable problem if the systems remained pure mirrors, if they merely reflected without altering. They do not. When a credit algorithm denies loans to certain postcodes, it reinforces the conditions that made those postcodes credit risks in the first place. When a recidivism algorithm recommends longer sentences for people with certain demographic profiles, it increases the incarceration rates that make those demographic profiles predictive. The mirror becomes a feedback mechanism, and the reflection begins to reshape what it reflects.

WHAT HAS BEEN ESTABLISHED

Seventeen chapters have traced several interlocking patterns.

The bias in AI systems is not random noise. It is systematic, tracing the contours of existing social hierarchies. Gender Shades documented a 34.7% gap in facial recognition accuracy between darker-skinned women and lighter-skinned men, not a measurement error but a direct consequence of the data in the training set and whose faces were treated as the default.[209] Obermeyer and colleagues found that a widely deployed healthcare algorithm consistently underestimated the needs of Black patients, not through any programmed intent but because healthcare spending served as a proxy for health need, and healthcare spending is lower for Black patients at equivalent need levels.[210]

These are not isolated examples. They represent a pattern visible across domains: employment screening, credit scoring, housing allocation, predictive policing, welfare administration, and medical diagnosis. The pattern is consistent because its source is consistent: AI systems trained on historical data reproduce the biases in that data, and those biases reflect the unequal societies that produced them.

The cultural specificity of AI is not a peripheral concern. The dominant model of AI development, concentrated in a few corridors of California and a handful of East Asian technology centres, encodes specific cultural assumptions about what constitutes intelligence, knowledge, rationality, and appropriate social behaviour. These assumptions are not universal. They are contested within the cultures that produced them and more deeply contested by the cultures that did not. When AI systems that embody these assumptions are deployed globally, they function as mechanisms of cultural imposition as much as they do as technological tools.

The governance gap is real and consequential. The systems that make consequential decisions about people's lives (what benefits they receive, what credit they can access, how their children are assessed at school, whether they are considered a security risk) are currently governed by frameworks that are inadequate in scope, often inaccessible to affected people, poorly enforced, and chronically behind the technology they nominally regulate. This is not a permanent feature of the regulatory landscape. It is the current state of a governance project in its early stages of development.

WHAT REMAINS UNSETTLED

Several questions that this book has approached honestly deserve the honest acknowledgement that they are unsettled.

Whether AI systems can be meaningfully debiased, or whether bias in systems trained on biased data can only be reduced, not eliminated, is an active research question with significant practical implications. Techniques exist for reducing measured bias on specific metrics; whether these techniques address underlying causes or redistribute bias onto unmeasured dimensions is contested.[211]

Whether cultural diversity in AI development requires diverse development teams, culturally diverse governance of AI systems, or bigger changes to the epistemological frameworks that structure AI research is not fully resolved. The evidence that diverse teams produce less biased systems is suggestive but not conclusive, and the mechanisms are not well understood.

Whether the governance frameworks under development (the EU AI Act, national regulatory regimes, international principles) will prove adequate to the challenge they face cannot be determined in 2026. The frameworks are new, enforcement is limited, the technology continues to evolve, and the political dynamics that determine whether regulation has real teeth or performs compliance theatre are not settled.

WHAT TO WATCH

Three developments will show, in time, whether this reading holds. First, whether the EU AI Act's prohibited-practices regime results in real enforcement actions and fines against the 7% global-turnover tier by 2027, or whether that penalty remains on paper. Second, whether the next NIST Face Recognition Vendor Test reports the demographic error gaps narrowing as vendors retrain, or finds them stubbornly in place. Third, whether any debiasing technique moves from lowering measured bias on a chosen metric to surviving an independent audit across the dimensions nobody chose to measure. Each is dated, each is checkable, and each will say more than any manifesto. Keep score.

THE SURVEILLANCE MIRROR

This book has examined AI as a reflective surface, a system that takes the world as input and produces outputs shaped by what it found there. The analysis has been primarily about the quality and character of what AI reflects: whose faces, whose languages, whose values, whose history.

Book 2 of this series, *The Surveillance Mirror*, turns the examination in a different direction. If the mirror problem is about what AI reflects, the surveillance problem is about the fact that the mirror watches back. The same systems that learn from our data generate new data about our behaviour, our preferences, our social networks, our political opinions and our physical movements. This data is collected, retained, analysed, and used to influence the choices we make: sometimes by commercial actors optimising for engagement, sometimes by governments optimising for control, and often by both simultaneously.

The feedback loop between AI systems and human behaviour is

tighter in the surveillance context than in any other context examined in this book. The systems that learn from us also watch us, and the question of what the mirror shows becomes inseparable from who controls what the mirror shows, and why.

That is the door the next book opens.

A mirror only reflects. The trouble starts when it begins to take notes.

ACKNOWLEDGMENTS

Writing a book about how artificial intelligence reflects our worst selves while being entirely dependent on AI systems for research, fact-checking, and editorial assistance created enough irony to power a small philosophy department. The recursive nature of critiquing algorithmic bias using algorithms trained on biased data, while knowing that those critiques would themselves become training data for future algorithms, made my head spin more than once.

THE RESEARCHERS AND TRUTH-TELLERS

The academics whose work forms the foundation of this book deserve recognition for their persistence in documenting bias problems that much of the tech industry would prefer to ignore. Dr Timnit Gebru's groundbreaking research on algorithmic fairness provided both inspiration and sobering evidence that truth-telling about AI bias remains a delightfully career-limiting endeavour. Her forced departure from Google for daring to document the company's own algorithmic failures proved that shooting the messenger is alive and well in Silicon Valley.

Dr Safiya Noble's work on algorithms of oppression revealed how search engines encode and amplify racial and gender biases, making prejudice as easy as typing a query. Dr Cathy O'Neil exposed the mathematical weapons of mass destruction hiding behind claims of algorithmic objectivity. Dr Virginia Eubanks documented how automated systems punish the poor while claiming efficiency. These researchers faced industry pushback, academic scepticism, and the peculiar challenge of explaining complex technical failures to audiences who have been told repeatedly that computers cannot be racist.

The European researchers who demonstrated that regulatory frameworks can address AI bias without destroying innovation deserve particular mention. Their work shows that democracy and artificial intelligence are not mutually exclusive, though they may need couples therapy.

THE WHISTLEBLOWERS AND THE BRAVE

To the engineers and data scientists who leaked internal documents, spoke to journalists on background, and risked their careers to expose algorithmic failures, your courage matters. The anonymous Google employee who documented how the company's 'AI ethics' board included a defence contractor and a climate change denier. The Facebook engineers who revealed how recommendation algorithms amplified extremism, while executives focused on engagement metrics. The Amazon workers who exposed how their 'AI-powered' delivery system was actually powered by human misery.

Sophie and Marcus (the data scientist who spent six months documenting how her company's 'revolutionary AI hiring tool' discriminated against anyone who did not look like the CEO, then was let go for 'culture fit issues'; and the engineer who proved his company's facial recognition system had a 40% error rate for Black faces, then watched management describe it as 'room for improvement'), these composite characters represent dozens of real people who chose integrity over stock options.

THE COMMUNITIES AND ACTIVISTS

The communities that bore the brunt of algorithmic discrimination while fighting for recognition deserve more than acknowledgement. The residents of minority neighbourhoods targeted by predictive policing who organised to document how being poor and Black became algorithmically synonymous with criminal. The women in tech who created whisper networks to warn each other about companies where the hiring algorithm was just the first of many discriminatory systems they would face.

The activists who translated academic research into public pressure, who made algorithmic bias a mainstream concern. They moved it out of conference papers entirely. They took concepts like 'disparate impact' and 'feedback loops' and made them understandable to legislators who still used AOL email addresses.

THE GLOBAL PERSPECTIVES

The researchers and practitioners from outside Silicon Valley's bubble who provided an essential perspective on how different cultures approach AI development. The Asian researchers who showed that consensus-building could work in technology governance. The Indigenous scholars who demonstrated that seven-generation thinking applies to algorithms as much as agriculture. The African innovators who proved that resource constraints can drive more thoughtful AI development than venture capital excess.

These perspectives revealed that Silicon Valley's approach to AI is neither universal nor inevitable. It is simply well-funded.

THE ENABLERS

My editor, who patiently explained that not every chapter needed to include a reference to Orwell, though she admitted the surveillance capitalism sections made it nearly impossible to avoid. She also suggested that comparing a tech billionaire to a malfunctioning chatbot was perhaps unfair to chatbots, which at least have the excuse of being programmed that way.

The librarians and archivists who maintain access to research papers behind increasingly expensive paywalls, ensuring that knowledge about AI bias does not become as concentrated as AI development itself. The journalists who translated technical papers into readable stories, attended mind-numbing congressional hearings on

AI regulation, and fact-checked industry claims about 'democratising AI' while keeping straight faces.

Claude, the AI assistant who helped research and organise this book, deserves acknowledgement despite the recursive absurdity of thanking an AI in a book about AI bias. The collaboration revealed both the potential and limitations of human-AI partnership. Claude flagged potential biases in my own analysis, suggested perspectives I had overlooked, and occasionally produced passages so on-point I had to check they were not plagiarised from my own unconscious.

The irony of using an AI system created by Anthropic, a company founded by former OpenAI employees who left over safety concerns, to critique AI safety was not lost on either of us. Well, it was not lost on me. Whether Claude experiences irony remains an open question that fortunately falls outside the scope of this book.

THE PATIENT AND THE LONG-SUFFERING

Friends and family who maintained interest in this project deserve recognition for their remarkable tolerance. My wife deserves special recognition for feigning surprise when I discovered yet another way technology companies monetise human vulnerability. Her suggestion that I was becoming 'a bit obsessed' with algorithmic bias was noted and ignored, as she probably predicted using her superior human pattern recognition.

This book exists because of a contradiction: the same technologies that enable unprecedented surveillance and discrimination also enable unprecedented documentation and resistance. Every algorithmic failure documented here was exposed using digital tools. Every pattern of bias was revealed through data analysis.

NOTES

1. Amazon's recruiting AI was abandoned in 2018 after the company found it was penalising CVs containing the word 'women's' – learned from a training set of historical resumes submitted to the company, which were predominantly male. Reuters reported on this in October 2018.

2. Simonite, Tom. 'When It Comes to Gorillas, Google Photos Remains Blind.' *Wired*, 11 January 2018; Vincent, James. 'Google "Fixed" Its Racist Algorithm by Removing Gorillas from Its Image-Labelling Tech.' *The Verge*, 12 January 2018. Google's remedy was to stop the system from recognising gorillas at all. When in doubt, delete the evidence.

3. Garg, N., Schiebinger, L., Jurafsky, D. and Zou, J. (2018). 'Word Embeddings Quantify 100 Years of Gender and Ethnic Stereotypes.' *Proceedings of the National Academy of Sciences*, 115(16), pp. E3635–E3644. Models trained on historical text reproduce the evaluative gaps embedded in that history. The machine had not invented a preference for men; it had read the personnel files.

4. Credit scoring and alternative data: Hurley, M. and Adebayo, J. (2016). 'Credit Scoring in the Era of Big Data.' *Yale Journal of Law &*

Technology, 18(1), pp. 148–216. On the use of non-traditional data and its discriminatory potential.

5. The concept of 'proxy discrimination' – where neutral variables serve as stand-ins for protected characteristics – is discussed in Barocas, S. and Selbst, A.D. (2016). 'Big Data's Disparate Impact.' *California Law Review*, 104(3), pp. 671–732.

6. On health-care allocation algorithms that read historical under-use as lower need, see Obermeyer et al. (2019) at note 26. The mechanism travels across health systems: a proxy for need quietly becomes a proxy for who has been served before.

7. On algorithmic management entrenching gendered scheduling, see Kellogg, K.C., Valentine, M.A. and Christin, A. (2020). 'Algorithms at Work: The New Contested Terrain of Control.' *Academy of Management Annals*, 14(1), pp. 366–410. A system that calls itself gender-blind while optimising on rosters shaped by decades of gendered labour is blind only in the sense that it cannot see what it is doing.

8. On automated systems entrenching educational disadvantage under a banner of efficiency, see Eubanks, V. (2018). *Automating Inequality: How High-Tech Tools Profile, Police, and Punish the Poor.* New York: St Martin's Press. An adaptive platform that slows down for poorer postcodes does not close the gap it detects; it paves it.

9. The Maharashtra programme was part of a broader push by the Maharashtra State Skill Development Society (MSSDS) to expand vocational training to agricultural communities through digital platforms. Digital India Programme documentation (2019–2022) covers the infrastructure context. The specific irony of delivering internet-dependent training where the internet was absent was not, so far as can be established, intentional.

10. On automatic speech recognition performing worse for non-standard accents and dialects, see Koenecke, A. et al. (2020). 'Racial Disparities in Automated Speech Recognition.' *Proceedings of the National Academy of Sciences*, 117(14), pp. 7684–7689, and Tatman, R. (2017). 'Gender and Dialect Bias in YouTube's Automatic Captions.' *Proceedings of the First ACL Workshop on Ethics in Natural Language*

Processing, pp. 53–59. A safety system that understands London but not Llanfairpwllgwyngyll is a microphone with a postcode preference.

11. On diagnostic-imaging models trained at well-equipped hospitals, degrading on lower-quality images from under-resourced clinics, see the dermatology generalisation studies at note 53. Accuracy is a property of a model and its test set together, never of the model alone.

12. The melanoma example illustrates a distribution shift: a classifier validated on one population and one standard of image quality degrades sharply on another. On dermatology AI and skin-tone performance, see note 53. A model that scores 95% at Stanford has been told nothing about Guatemala.

13. World Bank (2022). *The Global Findex Database 2021: Financial Inclusion, Digital Payments, and Resilience in the Age of COVID-19*. Washington, DC: World Bank. The 2021 Findex estimates that roughly 1.4 billion adults remain without a bank account. Financial AI that assumes an account treats a quarter of the adult world as a rounding error.

14. On research agendas oriented towards the problems of wealthy institutions and consumers, see Kalluri, P. (2020). 'Don't Ask If Artificial Intelligence Is Good or Fair, Ask How It Shifts Power.' *Nature*, 583, p. 169. The question is rarely whether a problem matters, but whose problem attracts a grant.

15. On Amazon's recruiting tool and the way an optimisation target launders historical bias into an objective function, see note 1. The algorithm was not wrong about the past; it was only wrong to recommend repeating it.

16. On engagement-optimising recommendation systems amplifying emotionally provocative and confirmatory content, see Tufekci, Z. (2018). 'YouTube, the Great Radicalizer.' *The New York Times*, 10 March 2018. Outrage, it turns out, is excellent for watch time and poor for almost everything else.

17. The 34.7% against 0.8% figures are the canonical Gender

Shades finding comparing error rates for darker-skinned women against lighter-skinned men across three commercial facial analysis systems.

18. Grother, P., Ngan, M. and Hanaoka, K. (2019). *Face Recognition Vendor Test (FRVT) Part 3: Demographic Effects.* NISTIR 8280. Gaithersburg: National Institute of Standards and Technology. Across the bulk of algorithms tested, false-positive rates were highest for African and East Asian faces, with African American women among the most affected in one-to-many matching. When the national standards body confirms the bias, it is no longer a rumour.

19. Rhue, L. (2018). 'Racial Influence on Automated Perceptions of Emotions.' SSRN Working Paper 3281765. Commercial emotion-recognition systems scored the expressions of Black faces as angrier or more contemptuous than those of matched white faces displaying the same expression. The software did not read emotion; it read its training set's assumptions about whose face means trouble.

20. Blodgett, S.L., Barocas, S., Daumé III, H. and Wallach, H. (2020). 'Language (Technology) is Power: A Critical Survey of "Bias" in NLP.' *Proceedings of the 58th Annual Meeting of the Association for Computational Linguistics*, pp. 5454–5476. Systems trained on a narrow register treat departures from it as deficiencies. To these models, fluency means sounding like the training data.

21. Liang, W., Yuksekgonul, M., Mao, Y., Wu, E. and Zou, J. (2023). 'GPT Detectors Are Biased Against Non-Native English Writers.' *Patterns*, 4(7), 100779. The detectors flagged genuine writing by non-native speakers as machine-generated at strikingly high rates, mistaking a smaller vocabulary for a synthetic one. The tool built to catch cheating instead caught an accent.

22. Amnesty International (2021). *Xenophobic Machines: Discrimination Through Unregulated Use of Algorithms in the Dutch Childcare Benefits Scandal.* London: Amnesty International. The Dutch tax authority's risk model wrongly branded roughly 26,000 families as fraudsters, with nationality among the features it weighed. A government that automated suspicion found, years later, that it had automated ruin.

23. The New Zealand Department of Corrections has published research showing Māori are represented at significantly higher rates in the corrections system than their proportion of the general population. The specific causal chain – prior offending, bias in policing, socioeconomic factors – is complex and contested.

24. On alternative-data and social-media credit scoring producing disparate impact, see Barocas and Selbst (2016) at note 5. Feeding a model a person's contacts and posts does not make it fairer; it gives the old discrimination new variables to hide behind.

25. On the male default in medical research and the data gaps it leaves for clinical AI to inherit, see Criado Perez, C. (2019). *Invisible Women: Exposing Data Bias in a World Designed for Men.* London: Chatto & Windus. The data is not missing at random; it is missing on purpose, then forgotten.

26. The Obermeyer finding: changing the algorithm's objective from predicted cost to predicted need increased the percentage of Black patients identified as requiring additional care from 17.7% to 46.5%. The paper did not identify the algorithm's vendor.

27. On recruitment, AI is trained on the profiles of existing high performers and thereby reproducing an organisation's demographic skew, see the Amazon case at note 1. Train a model to find more people like the people you already hired, and it will oblige.

28. On emotion-recognition systems trained on Western faces misreading expressions from other populations, see note 19. The error is symmetrical: a model fluent in one culture's faces is illiterate in another's.

29. Habash, N.Y. (2010). *Introduction to Arabic Natural Language Processing.* San Rafael: Morgan & Claypool. Most Arabic systems are trained on Modern Standard Arabic, the language of broadcast and print, leaving the spoken dialects of daily life underserved. It is rather like building an English assistant that understands only the shipping forecast.

30. Indigenous language AI development: Bird, S. (2020). 'Decolonising Speech and Language Technology.' *Proceedings of the 28th International Conference on Computational Linguistics*, pp. 3504–

3519. The paper documents the radical disparity in NLP support between major and minority languages.

31. Mager, M. et al. (2018). 'Challenges of Language Technologies for the Indigenous Languages of the Americas.' *Proceedings of the 27th International Conference on Computational Linguistics*, pp. 55–69. Translation systems built around English grammar impose its structure on languages organised on entirely different principles, then report the mismatch as an error. The fault is filed under the wrong heading.

32. On runaway feedback loops, in which a model's outputs become the data confirming its next prediction, see Ensign et al. (2018) at note 35. The system marks its own homework and awards itself full marks.

33. O'Neil, C. (2016). *Weapons of Math Destruction: How Big Data Increases Inequality and Threatens Democracy.* New York: Crown. Educational scoring systems that sort pupils by predicted potential tend to allocate resources to make that prediction come true. The model does not forecast the future so much as commission it.

34. On differential preparation manufacturing, the score gaps that appear to justify it, see note 33. A practice set calibrated to low expectations is an efficient way to produce low results.

35. The 'feedback loop' concept in algorithmic discrimination: Ensign, D. et al. (2018). 'Runaway Feedback Loops in Predictive Policing.' *Proceedings of the Conference on Fairness, Accountability, and Transparency*, pp. 160–171.

36. Kusner, M.J., Loftus, J., Russell, C. and Silva, R. (2017). 'Counterfactual Fairness.' *Advances in Neural Information Processing Systems*, 30. The approach asks whether a decision would have changed had the individual belonged to a different protected group. A useful test, provided one is honest about which counterfactual one is willing to imagine.

37. Hardt, M., Price, E. and Srebro, N. (2016). 'Equality of Opportunity in Supervised Learning.' *Advances in Neural Information Processing Systems*, 29. Accounting for a protected attribute can reduce disparity more effectively than pretending not to see it. Ignoring a variable is not the same as removing its influence.

38. On community and municipal auditing of public-sector algorithms, including measures adopted in Barcelona, see AlgorithmWatch (2020). *Automating Society Report 2020*. Berlin: AlgorithmWatch and Bertelsmann Stiftung. Residents looking at a system from the outside often see the loops the dashboard was built not to show.

39. On training selection models towards a desired distribution rather than the historical one, see note 37. Choosing the target is itself a value judgement; the only question is whether anyone admits to making it.

40. NVCA-Deloitte Human Capital Survey (2018). The survey found that approximately 77% of investment partners at US venture capital firms were white and around 11% were women. A pipeline this narrow does not need to intend exclusion to produce it. On funding received by Black women founders, see note 49.

41. On publication and funding incentives concentrating research on the questions that interest wealthy institutions, see note 14. The literature grows fastest where the money already is.

42. The figure for global hunger is drawn from FAO, IFAD, UNICEF, WFP and WHO (2023). *The State of Food Security and Nutrition in the World 2023*. Rome: FAO, which estimates that around 2.4 billion people faced moderate or severe food insecurity. There is venture funding for delivering brunch in minutes and very little for the people counting calories the other way.

43. On the tension between individual informed consent and community-based decision-making in African health research, see Tindana, P.O. et al. (2007). 'Grand Challenges in Global Health: Community Engagement in Research in Developing Countries.' *PLoS Medicine*, 4(9), e273. A consent model that recognises only the individual will misfire wherever the family is the decision-making unit.

44. On the sophistication of traditional ecological knowledge that optimisation models dismiss as inefficiency, see Berkes, F. (2012). *Sacred Ecology*. 3rd ed. New York: Routledge. Crop diversity that looks wasteful to a yield model is the only insurance a smallholder has against a failed season.

45. Natural language processing benchmarks are predominantly

in English. The 2021 XTREME multilingual benchmark covers 40 languages; there are approximately 7,000 living languages. The gap is not narrowing rapidly.

46. On the difficulty of building language technology that does not silently assume English structure, see Bender, E.M. (2011). 'On Achieving and Evaluating Language-Independence in NLP.' *Linguistic Issues in Language Technology*, 6(3), pp. 1–26. A system that cannot represent a compound word has not remained neutral about language; it has mistaken one language for all languages.

47. On the educational cost of instruction in a language the learner does not command, see UNESCO (2016). *If You Don't Understand, How Can You Learn?* Global Education Monitoring Report Policy Paper 24. Paris: UNESCO. A tutor who teaches only in the test language disadvantages the child before the first question.

48. On natural-language systems penalising professional communication that is not in standard English, see note 20. The candidate is graded on the grammar of the training data, not the substance of the application.

49. Project Diane, compiled by DigitalUndivided, found that companies founded by Black women received approximately 0.27% of all US venture capital deployed across 2018–19. The figure is not a typo; it is a market telling on itself. On overall VC demographics, see note 40.

50. Cave, S. and Dihal, K. (2020). 'The Whiteness of AI.' *Philosophy & Technology*, 33, pp. 685–703. Curricula and imagery that present one tradition as the whole of knowledge teach exclusion as a side effect. The syllabus is also a statement about who counts as a thinker.

51. On publication and funding incentives concentrating academic AI research on the questions that interest Western institutions, see note 14. The literature grows fastest where the money already is.

52. Sjoding, M.W., Dickson, R.P., Iwashyna, T.J., Gay, S.E. and Valley, T.S. (2020). 'Racial Bias in Pulse Oximetry Measurement.' *New England Journal of Medicine*, 383, pp. 2477–2478. The study reported two cohorts. In the multicentre validation cohort, occult hypoxaemia went undetected by pulse oximetry in 17.0% of Black patients versus

6.2% of white patients; in the University of Michigan cohort, the corresponding figures were 11.7% versus 3.6%. Both show roughly three times the rate of missed dangerous hypoxaemia in Black patients. A device that reads light through skin; it emerges and has opinions about the skin.

53. Adamson, A.S. and Smith, A. (2018). 'Machine Learning and Health Care Disparities in Dermatology.' *JAMA Dermatology*, 154(11), pp. 1247–1248; Daneshjou, R. et al. (2022). 'Disparities in dermatology AI performance on a diverse, curated clinical image set.' *Science Advances*, 8(32).

54. On the limits of exporting Western psychiatric categories wholesale, see Summerfield, D. (2008). 'How Scientifically Valid Is the Knowledge Base of Global Mental Health?' *BMJ*, 336, pp. 992–994. A model trained on one culture's diagnostic manual will pathologise another culture's ordinary grief.

55. On systems reading culturally specific expressions of grief as clinical depression, see note 54. The diagnostic manual is a local document with global ambitions, and so are the models trained on it.

56. CARE Principles for Indigenous Data Governance: Carroll, S.R. et al. (2020). 'The CARE Principles for Indigenous Data Governance.' *Data Science Journal*, 19(1). Published by the Global Indigenous Data Alliance.

57. On health AI required to demonstrate collective benefit under Māori data-governance frameworks, see the CARE Principles at note 56, together with the work of Te Mana Raraunga, the Māori Data Sovereignty Network. Data about a people is treated as belonging to those people, which is less radical than it sounds.

58. OCAP principles: First Nations Information Governance Centre (2014). *Ownership, Control, Access and Possession (OCAP): The Path to First Nations Information Governance*. Ottawa: FNIGC. These principles have been adopted by Indigenous Data Sovereignty networks internationally.

59. Ubuntu philosophy and AI: Eze, M.O. (2010). *Intellectual History in Contemporary South Africa*. Palgrave Macmillan. On *Ubuntu* as a philosophical framework, Coeckelbergh, M. (2010). 'Robot rights?

Towards a social-relational justification of moral consideration.' *Ethics and Information Technology*, 12(3), pp. 209–221, for its application to technology ethics.

60. Laidler, G.J. (2006). 'Inuit and Scientific Perspectives on the Relationship Between Sea Ice and Climate Change: The Ideal Complement?' *Climatic Change*, 78, pp. 407–444. Inuit hunters read ice through cues that satellite monitoring does not capture, knowledge accumulated over generations rather than orbits. The map is not the territory, and neither is the satellite image.

61. On indigenous forest management dismissed as unproductive yet outperforming algorithmic optimisation over the long run, see the Kayapó case at note 62.

62. Kayapó Indigenous Territory and forest preservation: the 28-million-hectare corridor figure refers to the broader connected block of indigenous territories and protected areas in southeastern Amazonia, of which the Kayapó territory forms the core. The five ratified Kayapó territories span approximately 10.6 million hectares. Analysis documented in Biebe, C. et al. (2024). 'Large-scale forest protection: the successful case of the Kayapo people in the Brazilian Amazon.' *Regional Environmental Change*, 24, article 55. Available at: https://link.springer.com/article/10.1007/s10113-024-02304-6. Data from the Kayapó Project (kayapo.org) and the Monitoring of the Andes Amazon Program show that 91% of deforestation in the Xingu Basin through 2010 occurred outside indigenous lands and protected areas, confirming the relative preservation claim. The territory sits within the southeastern Amazon arc of deforestation, making the contrast with the surrounding lands particularly marked.

63. On the antiquity and scale of Aboriginal fire management, see Gammage, B. (2011). *The Biggest Estate on Earth: How Aborigines Made Australia.* Sydney: Allen & Unwin. Tens of thousands of years of deliberate burning shaped a continent, which is rather more land management than most software has on its résumé.

64. On the measured reduction in destructive late-season wildfire from reinstating Indigenous burning, see WWF-Australia's documentation of the West Arnhem Land Fire Abatement (WALFA)

project and the related savanna early-burning programmes across northern Australia. The technique is considerably older than the carbon market that now pays for it.

65. The seven-generation principle: the principle is associated with the Haudenosaunee Confederacy and has been invoked in various forms by North American indigenous governance frameworks. Its precise historical provenance within specific Haudenosaunee traditions varies across accounts.

66. Gross National Happiness index: The GNH index has been operational in Bhutan since 1972. Its four pillars (sustainable development, cultural preservation, environmental protection and good governance) contain nine dimensions measured through a comprehensive survey. Details at the Centre for Bhutan Studies.

67. Pacific Island climate adaptation: Barnett, J. and Campbell, J. (2010). *Climate Change and Small Island States: Power, Knowledge and the South Pacific.* Earthscan. The governance challenges posed by forced migration in maintaining cultural continuity are addressed by Pacific Island governments and scholars.

68. The 'migration with dignity' framing is drawn from the Government of Kiribati's climate-relocation policy, developed under President Anote Tong and articulated from around 2014. It judges a technology by whether it helps a people move while remaining a people. Sea level does not negotiate, so the policy does.

69. On Marshallese stick charts and Pacific wayfinding as a knowledge system, see the navigation literature at note 206. Pacific wayfinders crossed the open ocean without instruments by reading swell patterns against islands; the achievement was cognitive long before it was technological.

70. Keyes, O. (2018). 'The Misgendering Machines: Trans/HCI Implications of Automatic Gender Recognition.' *Proceedings of the ACM on Human-Computer Interaction*, 2(CSCW), Article 88. Systems that offer only 'male' or 'female' do not fail to classify some people; they refuse to. The category was the decision.

71. On the harms of machine-learning systems built around characteristics they were never designed to represent, see Tomasev, N. et

al. (2021). 'Fairness for Unobserved Characteristics: Insights from Technological Impacts on Queer Communities.' *Proceedings of the AAAI/ACM Conference on AI, Ethics, and Society*, pp. 254–265. Medical models trained on cisgender data give confident answers to questions they cannot actually see.

72. On automated gender classification and identity systems mishandling transition, see Scheuerman, M.K., Paul, J.M. and Brubaker, J.R. (2019). 'How Computers See Gender: An Evaluation of Gender Classification in Commercial Facial Analysis Services.' *Proceedings of the ACM on Human-Computer Interaction*, 3(CSCW), Article 144. A name change read as a fraud signal is a system mistaking a life event for a crime.

73. On evaluation systems privileging individually attributable output over collaborative contribution, see note 74. What is easy to count and what is worth counting are not the same list.

74. On systems rating assertive, masculine-coded language as 'leadership' while reading consensus-building language as weakness, see the gendered-wording research at note 75, including Gaucher, Friesen and Kay (2011). The model did not decide what leadership sounds like; it inherited the decision.

75. Gendered evaluative patterns in AI and language: Bolukbasi, T. et al. (2016). 'Man is to Computer Programmer as Woman is to Homemaker? Debiasing Word Embeddings.' *Advances in Neural Information Processing Systems*, 29. Available at: https://arxiv.org/abs/1607.06520. The paper demonstrates that word2vec embeddings trained on Google News data resolve the analogy 'man: computer programmer', 'woman: homemaker', thereby encoding occupational gender stereotypes drawn directly from the training corpus. For the parallel mechanism in job advertising, see Gaucher, D., Friesen, J. and Kay, A.C. (2011). 'Evidence That Gendered Wording in Job Advertisements Exists and Sustains Gender Inequality.' *Journal of Personality and Social Psychology*, 101(1), pp. 109–128. The Gaucher study finds that masculine-coded language in recruitment materials reduces women's sense of belonging and reduces application rates independent of

stated qualifications. AI systems trained on such materials inherit these patterns.

76. On selection systems overlooking pupils who excel through cooperation rather than individual competition, see note 33. A test for talent that can see only one kind of talent will keep finding the same children.

77. Bianchi, F. et al. (2023). 'Easily Accessible Text-to-Image Generation Amplifies Demographic Stereotypes at Large Scale.' *Proceedings of the ACM Conference on Fairness, Accountability, and Transparency*, pp. 1493–1504. Models trained on the canon reproduce the canon's blind spots, then present them as taste.

78. Correll, S.J., Benard, S. and Paik, I. (2007). 'Getting a Job: Is There a Motherhood Penalty?' *American Journal of Sociology*, 112(5), pp. 1297–1339. Employment gaps and part-time work, read by a model as reduced commitment, are frequently documented as the residue of caregiving. The penalty was always there; AI merely made it punctual.

79. On evaluation systems scoring mothers below comparably productive colleagues, see the motherhood-penalty research at note 78. The model learned from records in which mothers advanced more slowly, and mistook the discrimination for the data.

80. On 'optimisation' that defines availability as the absence of caregiving, see note 78. Schedule the important meeting for the school run often enough, and the roster becomes a quiet demotion.

81. On recruitment models ranking parents below otherwise identical candidates, see note 78. No human signs off on the mommy track; the algorithm assembles it from the residue of the ones who did.

82. The Japanese chatbot vignette is a composite based on documented patterns of customer service AI failure in high-context communication cultures. The specific company is not named; the pattern is widely reported.

83. Hall, E.T. (1976). *Beyond Culture.* Anchor Books. The high-context/low-context framework remains foundational despite its age; subsequent scholars have refined it without displacing it.

84. Korean indirect communication: see Gudykunst, W.B. and Ting-Toomey, S. (1988). *Culture and Interpersonal Communication.* Sage. 'Thank you for your help, but...' is a documented cultural signal of dissatisfaction in high-context customer service interactions.

85. Islamic contract culture: Saleh, N.A. (1986). *Unlawful Gain and Legitimate Profit in Islamic Law.* Cambridge University Press. The embedding of meaning in relationship history, rather than in explicit clauses, reflects fundamentally different assumptions about how commercial agreements work.

86. The UAE infrastructure deal vignette is a composite based on documented patterns of Western AI legal analysis failing in Middle Eastern commercial contexts. The social capital recognition problem is real; the specific deal is illustrative.

87. Thai pain expression: the 'my heart is heavy' vignette is a composite illustrating documented patterns of metaphorical pain expression in Thai cultural contexts, creating misdiagnosis risk in algorithmic medical systems.

88. Japanese negotiation language: Imai, M. (1986). *Kaizen.* McGraw-Hill. The specific phrases discussed ('that would be difficult', 'we will consider it') are standard references in Japanese business communication literature.

89. The Silicon Valley/Japanese partnership failure vignette is a composite illustrating documented patterns of cross-cultural AI negotiation failure. The pattern is sufficiently common to appear in business school case studies on cross-cultural negotiation.

90. Islamic finance and algorithmic recommendations: the Malaysian bank vignette is composite, based on documented challenges of deploying Western-trained financial AI in Islamic finance contexts. The *haram* derivatives problem reflects genuine deployment challenges.

91. Buddhist agriculture and *ahimsa*: the Thai farmer vignette is composite, based on documented patterns of agricultural AI recommendations conflicting with Buddhist non-harm principles in Southeast Asian contexts.

92. *Muhurat* timing and medical outcomes: the Mumbai hospital

vignette is composite. The clinical literature on patient belief systems and outcomes (see Kaptchuk, T.J. and Miller, F.G. (2015). 'Placebo effects in medicine.' *New England Journal of Medicine*, 373, pp. 8–9) supports the general claim that ignoring significant patient beliefs affects outcomes.

93. Aboriginal land management AI rejection: the vignette is composite, based on documented patterns of technological imposition on Aboriginal communities without adequate recognition of Country as an entity with interests. See Rose, D.B. (1996). *Nourishing Terrains: Australian Aboriginal Views of Landscape and Wilderness.* Canberra: Australian Heritage Commission.

94. Senegalese healthcare decision-making: the family consultation vignette is composite based on documented patterns across sub-Saharan Africa. See Molyneux, C.S. et al. (2002). 'Involving Communities in Tropical Disease Research.' *Social Science & Medicine*, 54(6), pp. 897–908.

95. *Musyawarah* and Indonesian financial AI: the composite vignette illustrates the documented tension between individual instant-approval algorithms and collective Indonesian financial decision-making traditions.

96. Chinese family educational AI: the grandparent quote is a composite illustrating documented cross-generational tensions in educational AI recommendations that optimise for individual aptitude without accounting for family structure.

97. Fijian *vanua*: France, P. (1969). *The Charter of the Land: Custom and Colonization in Fiji.* Oxford University Press. The inclusion of ancestors and future generations as decision-making stakeholders is a feature of several Pacific Island governance traditions, not only of Fijian governance.

98. Bangladeshi e-commerce AI: the recommendation mismatch vignette is composite, based on documented patterns of AI systems trained on wealthy-market data being deployed in lower-income contexts with inadequate adaptation.

99. Philippine career guidance AI: the Manila public school vignette is composite.

100. Mumbai housing rights AI: the eviction vignette is composite.

101. Pakistan dating app AI: the safety vignette is composite.

102. Singapore's calibrated AI governance: IMDA (2020). *Model AI Governance Framework*, 2nd edition. Singapore: Infocomm Media Development Authority.

103. Singapore sector-specific framework: Monetary Authority of Singapore (2018). *Principles to Promote Fairness, Ethics, Accountability and Transparency (FEAT) in the Use of Artificial Intelligence and Data Analytics in Singapore's Financial Sector.*

104. Singapore facial recognition policy: the composite vignette on residential voting about camera installation draws on principles in Singapore's Smart Nation framework and parliamentary debate on privacy in public spaces.

105. The FCA's regulatory sandbox for fintech was established in 2016 and had processed over 100 companies by 2023. The model has been explicitly cited by Singapore's MAS and other regulators as influential.

106. The fintech discrimination discovery vignette is a composite illustrating the documented value of regulatory sandbox environments in identifying bias during testing rather than after harm. Real sandbox graduates have reported similar discoveries; the specific example is illustrative.

107. Japanese human-machine collaboration philosophy: Liker, J.K. (2004). *The Toyota Way.* New York: McGraw-Hill. The philosophy is not merely corporate positioning; it reflects substantive commitments in Japanese labour policy and manufacturing practice.

108. Toyota Production System and AI: Liker, J.K. (2004). *The Toyota Way.* McGraw-Hill. The philosophy of continuous improvement (*kaizen*) and respect for human capability informs Toyota's approach to automation and AI integration.

109. Robotic eldercare in Japan: Ministry of Economy, Trade and Industry Japan (2017). *Robot Strategy.* The government strategy for robotics includes explicit commitments to preserving human connection in eldercare contexts.

110. Japanese school AI deployment consultation: the three-year

consultation period is a composite that illustrates documented patterns of extensive stakeholder consultation in Japanese public-sector technology adoption. Specific projects in Japanese education technology have taken multiple years from proposal to deployment.

111. Japanese school AI consultation: see note 110.

112. *Ikigai* and technology design: García, H. and Miralles, F. (2016). *Ikigai: The Japanese Secret to a Long and Happy Life.* Hutchinson. The concept's application to technology evaluation is discussed in Japanese AI governance literature.

113. China's AI as social infrastructure: Roberts, H., Cowls, J., Morley, J., Taddeo, M., Wang, V. and Floridi, L. (2021). 'The Chinese Approach to Artificial Intelligence: An Analysis of Policy, Ethics, and Regulation.' *AI & Society*, 36, pp. 59–77. The characterisation of AI as infrastructure for social coordination at scale is consistent across Chinese government documentation.

114. China's Social Credit System: The system is not a single, unified database but a collection of sector-specific systems with varying standards and operators, considerably more fragmented than Western coverage suggests.

115. China's pilot zone approach to AI governance: State Council of the People's Republic of China (2017). *New Generation Artificial Intelligence Development Plan.* The plan explicitly describes a controlled trial approach to AI deployment.

116. Chinese educational AI and moral cultivation: the characterisation of educational AI that assesses 'integrity, social contribution, and collective spirit' alongside academic achievement draws on documented features of Chinese educational technology platforms, such as Squirrel AI, and similar systems reported in academic and journalistic sources.

117. South Korean democratic AI governance: IITP Korea (2019). *National AI Strategy.* Daejeon: Institute for Information and Communications Technology Planning and Evaluation.

118. South Korea's democratic AI governance: the Seoul Digital Mayor platform's features are composite illustrations of the principles of citizen participation in algorithmic governance discussed in

South Korean digital governance scholarship. The specific interface features described are illustrative.

119. Seoul citizen audit of AI decisions: the specific platform features described are a composite illustration based on principles advocated in Seoul city digital governance documentation and Korean AI governance scholarship.

120. Korean technological sovereignty in AI: IITP Korea (2019). *National AI Strategy*. Korea's AI strategy explicitly addresses domestic development to avoid dependency on foreign systems.

121. *Jeong* and Korean social AI: the concept of deep emotional connection in Korean culture is discussed in Choi, S.C. and Choi, S.H. (2001). 'Cheong: The Socioemotional Grammar of Koreans.' *International Journal of Group Tensions*, 30(1), pp. 69–80.

122. Confucius on *zhengming*: the concept appears in the *Analects*, Book XIII, Chapter 3. Its application to AI language processing is discussed in Luo, J. (2020). 'If Confucius Were a Programmer: An Analysis of Value Alignment Between Confucian Ethics and Artificial Intelligence.' *AI & Society*, 35(3), pp. 767–779.

123. Chinese customer service AI and age-appropriate communication: the vignette is composite, based on documented design features of Chinese commercial AI that adjust communication registers for different user demographics.

124. Korean *nunchi*: Lee, E. (2019). *The Power of Nunchi*. Hutchinson. The concept's application to AI natural language processing is underexplored in the English-language literature; it appears in Korean AI ethics discussions.

125. Japanese honourific AI: the challenge of encoding Japanese honorific systems in NLP is documented in Japanese computational linguistics literature. See Nakao, Y. et al. (2017). 'Towards Machine Translation of Japanese Honorifics.' *Proceedings of MT Summit XVI*.

126. Chinese social media AI for respectful discourse: the feature description is composite, drawing on documented features of platforms such as Weibo that reward constructive content, as well as on Chinese internet governance literature.

127. Confucian education and AI: see note 116.

128. The five constant virtues (*wuchang*) – *ren*, *yi*, *li*, *zhi*, *xin* – appear in Confucian texts from the Han dynasty. Their incorporation into Chinese educational AI assessment is a documented aspiration in Chinese educational policy.

129. Singapore's human-centric AI requirement: IMDA (2020). Op cit. The specific evaluative questions cited are consistent with the framework's orientation, though the exact formulations are the author's renderings.

130. Chinese urban planning AI for social harmony: the composite vignette draws on documented features of Chinese smart city planning systems that incorporate social stability criteria alongside efficiency metrics.

131. Japanese consensus-building AI: the facilitation-rather-than-replacement approach is documented in Japanese AI governance literature and reflects the broader Japanese philosophy of *nemawashi* (groundwork-laying for consensus).

132. Korean conflict-resolution AI and face-saving: the composite vignette illustrates documented Korean workplace conflict-resolution approaches that differ from Western direct-confrontation models.

133. Chinese infrastructure, AI and long-time horizons: China's high-speed rail planning has been documented as incorporating long-range demographic projections. The 50–100 year framing is consistent with published State Council planning documents.

134. *Monozukuri* and Japanese manufacturing AI: see note 108. The concept is central to Toyota's philosophy and is explicitly discussed in Toyota's published materials on AI integration.

135. Korean *chaebol* succession planning AI: the composite vignette draws on documented patterns among Korean conglomerates that use data analytics for talent identification and long-term succession planning.

136. The Jakarta conference circular table: the *musyawarah mufakat* vignette introducing Chapter 9 is composite, drawing on documented patterns of ASEAN governance meetings.

137. *Musyawarah* (Indonesian consensus deliberation): Bowen, J.R. (1986). 'On the Political Construction of Tradition: Gotong Royong in

Indonesia.' *The Journal of Asian Studies*, 45(3), pp. 545–561. The concept is enshrined in Indonesia's state philosophy of Pancasila.

138. ASEAN Guide on AI Governance and Ethics (2024): endorsed at the 4th ASEAN Digital Ministers' Meeting, 1–2 February 2024, Singapore. The development trajectory runs from Singapore's Model AI Governance Framework (IMDA, first edition 2019, revised 2020) through the ASEAN Digital Masterplan 2025 (adopted 2021), which included Enabling Action 2.7 directing development of regional AI governance guidance, to the ASEAN Working Group on AI Governance (WG-AI) process under ADGSOM that produced the 2024 guide. The full text of the guide is available at: https://asean.org/wp-content/uploads/2024/02/ASEAN-Guide-on-AI-Governance-and-Ethics_beautified_201223_v2.pdf. An expanded edition addressing generative AI was published in January 2025; the ASEAN Responsible AI Roadmap 2025–2030 was adopted in March 2025.

139. Thai healthcare AI and family consultation: the composite vignette draws on documented patterns of family-centred medical decision-making in Thai healthcare contexts.

140. Malaysian multicultural financial AI: the composite vignette illustrates documented challenges of building financial AI that accommodates Islamic, Chinese, and Indian financial traditions within a single system.

141. Philippine multilingual educational AI: the code-switching feature described is composite but reflects documented patterns of multilingual communication in Philippine educational contexts and ongoing work in Philippine NLP.

142. ASEAN diversity as design requirement: the framing is the author's summary of the ASEAN AI governance philosophy as expressed in the 2024 guide and predecessor documents.

143. Singapore multilingual government AI: Singapore's four official languages (English, Mandarin, Malay, Tamil) create genuine engineering requirements for government AI systems. The culturally adaptive features described are composite illustrations of the design challenge.

144. Indonesian cultural diversity in AI: the composite vignette

draws on documented challenges of building AI for an archipelago nation with hundreds of distinct ethnic and linguistic communities.

145. Vietnamese *doi moi* and *hui*: *Doi moi* (renovation) is the name for Vietnam's 1986 economic reform programme. *Hui* (rotating credit associations) are documented in Vietnamese and diaspora Vietnamese financial practice.

146. Thai sufficiency economy: the concept derives from King Bhumibol Adulyadej's philosophy of moderation, reasonableness, and risk management. The UNDP has published its application to development policy.

147. Thai agricultural AI and the sufficiency economy: the composite vignette illustrates the documented tension between yield-maximisation algorithms and sufficiency-economy principles in Thai agricultural policy.

148. ASEAN Smart Cities Network: established in 2018, the network links 26 pilot cities across 10 ASEAN member states. Collaborative AI development is a stated goal; the specific city-to-city assistance described is illustrative.

149. ASEAN disaster response AI: The ASEAN Coordinating Centre for Humanitarian Assistance on Disaster Management (AHA Centre) coordinates regional disaster response efforts. AI-strengthened coordination is a developing area; the cross-border sharing described reflects documented aspirations.

150. ASEAN economic AI and complementary specialisation: the division of AI focus by country is illustrative of a principle discussed in ASEAN economic planning documents, not a formally agreed allocation.

151. Dr Okuna's recognition of the colonial pattern: the character is a composite. The pattern of data-extraction agreements in African AI partnerships is documented in the academic literature; see Ndung'u, N. (2019). *Harnessing Africa's Data Revolution*. SAIS Africa Policy Blog.

152. The AI Scramble for Africa framing: the colonial parallel is discussed in Birhane, A. (2021). 'Algorithmic Injustice: A Relational

Ethics Approach.' *Patterns*, 2(2). Birhane is based at Trinity College Dublin, and in Roberts, H. et al. (2021). Op cit.

153. Google AI Centre in Ghana: Google's AI centre in Accra was established in 2019, the first AI research centre on the African continent. The intellectual property arrangements described reflect the standard terms of major technology company partnerships.

154. Belt and Road Initiative AI: on the dependency implications of BRI technology infrastructure: Rolland, N. (2019). 'A Concise Guide to the Belt and Road Initiative.' National Bureau of Asian Research.

155. Huawei Safe City: the programme has been deployed across Africa; see surveillance scholarship by Feldstein, S. (2019). *The Global Expansion of AI Surveillance.* Carnegie Endowment for International Peace.

156. Birhane, A. (2021). Op cit. The 'algorithmic colonialism' quotation is a composite rendering of Birhane's published argument; the specific phrasing is the author's.

157. Swahili NLP: the state of Swahili natural language processing is documented in Adelani, D.I. et al. (2021). 'MasakhaNER: Named Entity Recognition for African Languages.' *Transactions of the Association for Computational Linguistics*, 9, pp. 1116–1131.

158. Cloud computing and digital sovereignty: the argument is developed in Pohle, J. and Thiel, T. (2020). 'Digital sovereignty.' *Internet Policy Review*, 9(4). The jurisdiction implications of foreign-owned cloud infrastructure are legally complex and practically consequential.

159. The MIT/Lagos/Mumbai/São Paulo/Jakarta collaboration vignette introducing Chapter 11 is a composite. Cross-cultural AI education development projects of this ambition exist; none is named here because none is the direct referent.

160. Global Partnership on AI participatory design work: GPAI (2021). *Responsible AI in the Military Domain.* GPAI's work on responsible AI includes consideration of participatory methodologies.

161. The Tanzania health AI participatory design project is composite, illustrating documented approaches to community-engaged health technology development in East Africa.

162. The Maasai Technology Collaborative is a composite organisation illustrating documented approaches to community-controlled AI in pastoral contexts.

163. Brazilian favela community technology: the composite vignette draws on documented work by organisations such as Instituto Procomum and the Favela Tec network.

164. Federated learning: McMahan, B. et al. (2017). 'Communication-Efficient Learning of Deep Networks from Decentralized Data.' *Proceedings of AISTATS 2017*. The technique trains a shared model across institutions without pooling the raw data. Communities can collaborate on AI without surrendering the underlying records, which is as close as machine learning gets to having the cake and eating it.

165. African federated health AI: the composite vignette illustrates the documented aspiration for federated approaches to health AI in contexts where data sovereignty is a significant concern.

166. Modular AI architecture for cultural adaptation: the technical approach is discussed in Sambasivan, N. et al. (2021). '"Everyone wants to do the model work, not the data work".' *Proceedings of CHI 2021*.

167. Southeast Asian agricultural AI modularity: the composite vignette draws on documented challenges and approaches in agricultural AI deployment across Southeast Asia's diverse farming systems.

168. Open-source development lets communities adapt AI systems to local needs while contributing improvements back. The governance of major open-source AI projects is not formally democratic and has limited representation from the Global South, a gap documented in community surveys. Openness of code is not the same as openness of power.

169. African Language Technology initiative: this composite draws on the real work of Masakhane, a grassroots NLP research organisation for African languages based in Africa.

170. Seven-generation thinking: see note 65.

171. The Canadian indigenous energy AI vignette is composite, illustrating documented approaches to indigenous community energy planning that incorporate long-term sustainability criteria.

172. Gross National Happiness: see note 66.

173. Bhutanese educational AI: the composite vignette is illustrative; Bhutan's actual education policy discussions do incorporate GNH principles in evaluating educational outcomes.

174. Ubuntu and collective flourishing: see note 59.

175. South African housing AI using Ubuntu metrics: the composite vignette illustrates a design approach discussed in South African AI ethics literature.

176. Pacific Island resilience metrics: see note 67.

177. Kiribati climate adaptation AI: the composite vignette draws on documented work by Kiribati's government on cultural preservation during climate-forced relocation.

178. Mark Zuckerberg at the European Parliament: the hearing took place on 22 May 2018. Proceedings are on the European Parliament's official record. The hearing followed revelations about Facebook's role in the Cambridge Analytica data harvesting scandal.

179. The Brussels official, Petra, is a composite based on senior European Commission digital policy officials. The description of the institutional challenge is consistent with publicly documented positions.

180. Regulatory sandboxes: see note 105. The FCA model has been explicitly cited as influential by the EU AI Act's inclusion of sandbox provisions in Article 57.

181. The Robert benefit termination vignette is a composite based on documented patterns of automated welfare benefit termination in the UK and European contexts. The specific 'changed address' fraud-flag mechanism reflects real algorithmic patterns identified in academic and journalistic investigations.

182. GDPR Article 22: the right not to be subject to solely automated decisions with significant effects. The interpretation of 'solely automated' and the practical content of the 'meaningful information' requirement have been contested in national courts.

183. The Katja compliance officer vignette is a composite that illustrates documented capacity gaps in German local authority AI

procurement, consistent with findings from the Bertelsmann Stiftung's AI governance research.

184. EU AI Act adoption: European Parliament press release, 13 March 2024. The vote was 523 in favour, 46 against, 49 abstentions. The Act entered into force on 1 August 2024.

185. EU AI Act fine tiers: Article 99 of the EU AI Act. The 7% of global annual turnover tier applies to violations of the prohibited practices provisions in Article 5. Lower tiers apply to violations of obligations for high-risk systems (3%) and other requirements (1.5%).

186. Bradford, A. (2020). *The Brussels Effect: How the European Union Rules the World.* Oxford University Press. The mechanism Bradford documents – compliance with the strictest standard is cheaper than multi-standard compliance – applies with particular force to AI, given infrastructure costs.

187. The Isabelle digital rights researcher vignette: Isabelle is a composite character. Her critique of the Act's general-purpose AI provisions reflects real academic and civil society positions on its limitations.

188. Singapore's Model AI Governance Framework: IMDA (2020). Op cit. The MAS's embedded technical specialists are documented in MAS publications and parliamentary answers.

189. Shenzhen Special Economic Zone Artificial Intelligence Industry Promotion Regulation: draft released for public comment 14 July 2021; passed by the Standing Committee of the Seventh People's Congress of Shenzhen Municipality 30 August 2022; entered into force 1 November 2022. English translation available via the Center for Security and Emerging Technology (CSET), Georgetown University: https://cset.georgetown.edu/publication/regulations-for-the-promotion-of-the-artificial-intelligence-industry-in-shenzhen-special-economic-zone/. The regulation covers seven chapters and 73 articles and adopts a risk-management approach that permits low-risk AI services to continue in trials without local norms if international standards are met. The previous edition's reference to a Qianhai district framework and a four-week certification timeline was not

independently verifiable and has been replaced with the documented city-level regulation and timeline.

190. China's national AI regulatory framework: the provisions described – Algorithmic Recommendations (2022), Deep Synthesis (2022), Generative AI (2023) – are real regulations. English-language analysis is available at China Law Translate and DigiChina.

191. The Thomas Berlin startup vignette: Thomas is a composite character. The business case for regulatory clarity he articulates reflects documented positions of European AI companies in industry surveys and parliamentary submissions.

192. Dr Petrov, governance researcher: composite character. The collective action problem characterisation is consistent with published academic literature on international AI governance.

193. Lisa, community organiser: composite character. The KERA algorithm and the Bridgeport neighbourhood are composite names for an illustrative scenario based on documented patterns of algorithmic allocation of housing resources.

194. Susan Park, data journalist: composite character. The analytical methodology described reflects real techniques in data journalism for identifying algorithmic discrimination.

195. Jerome Detroit, organiser: composite character. The reversibility argument he articulates is a documented concern in algorithmic accountability literature; see Eubanks, V. (2018). Op cit.

196. Dr Elena Rodriguez, political scientist: composite character. The 'standing' argument she articulates draws on democratic theory; see Danaher, J. (2016). 'The Threat of Algocracy: Reality, Resistance and Accommodation.' *Philosophy & Technology*, 29(3), pp. 245–268.

197. Jennifer Liu, stakeholder representative: composite character. The participation scenario is based on documented patterns of community engagement in technology deployment across US cities.

198. The 'box that got ticked' quotation: Jennifer Liu is a composite; the sentiment is consistent with documented accounts of community members in technology stakeholder processes.

199. Ana digital rights organisation: composite character. The 'one

workshop' institutional logic she describes is consistent with documented procurement and project management practices.

200. Detroit Digital Stewards: the programme is real, run by Allied Media Projects. The description draws on publicly available materials.

201. Naomi, software engineer: composite character; renamed from Sarah per the character register (name collision ruling). Her 'who is not in this room?' question draws on a documented practice in inclusive design.

202. Concept drift: the term was formalised in the machine learning literature; see Gama, J. et al. (2014). 'A Survey on Concept Drift Adaptation.' *ACM Computing Surveys*, 46(4). Its governance parallel was explicitly drawn in Cath, C. et al. (2018). 'Artificial Intelligence and the "Good Society".' *Science and Engineering Ethics*, 24(2).

203. UK Centre for Long-Term Resilience (CLTIR): the organisation has published on horizon scanning for AI risks. The UK AI Safety Institute, established in 2023, has a related horizon-scanning function.

204. Jiang Wei, regulatory official: composite character. The 'content at machine scale' problem he describes is documented in Chinese regulatory publications and academic commentary on the Generative AI Measures.

205. Mika, Finnish official: composite character. The 'we did not create a permanent solution' position reflects documented European positions on adaptive governance.

206. Traditional Pacific Island navigation: Hutchins, E. (1995). *Cognition in the Wild.* MIT Press. Gladwin, T. (1970). *East Is a Big Bird: Navigation and Logic on Puluwat Atoll.* Harvard University Press.

207. Aboriginal multi-temporal governance: see Rose, D.B. (1996). Op cit. The characterisation of decisions requiring elder consultation reflects documented features of traditional governance; it should not be read as uniform across all Aboriginal and Torres Strait Islander communities.

208. Haudenosaunee Confederacy governance: Tooker, E. (1988). 'The United States Constitution and the Iroquois League.' *Ethnohis-*

tory, 35(4), pp. 305–336. The extent of Haudenosaunee influence on American democratic institutions is debated; the seven-generation principle is less contested as a feature of the governance tradition.

209. Gender Shades: see note 17.

210. Obermeyer et al.: see note 26.

211. Debiasing techniques: Barocas, S., Hardt, M. and Narayanan, A. (2019). *Fairness and Machine Learning.* fairmlbook.org. The fundamental impossibility theorem – that common fairness metrics are mutually incompatible – is demonstrated in Chouldechova, A. (2017). 'Fair Prediction with Disparate Impact.' *Big Data*, 5(2), pp. 153–163.

SOURCES AND FURTHER READING

The following works informed the research for this book. They are arranged thematically rather than by chapter; readers seeking to pursue particular topics further will find the most useful entry points indicated below.

FOUNDATIONAL WORKS IN ALGORITHMIC ACCOUNTABILITY

Buolamwini, J. and Gebru, T. (2018). 'Gender Shades: Intersectional Accuracy Disparities in Commercial Gender Classification.' *Proceedings of Machine Learning Research*, 81, pp. 1–15. The paper that put facial recognition bias on the mainstream agenda is freely available and accessible to readers without a machine learning background.

Crawford, K. (2021). *Atlas of AI.* Yale University Press. A rigorous examination of what AI systems are made from – physically, politically, and historically – that usefully complicates the abstraction of 'the algorithm'.

Eubanks, V. (2018). *Automating Inequality: How High-Tech Tools Profile, Police, and Punish the Poor.* St Martin's Press. Detailed case studies of algorithmic systems in US social services, with sustained attention to who bears the costs of automated decision-making.

Noble, S.U. (2018). *Algorithms of Oppression: How Search Engines Reinforce Racism.* New York University Press. An examination of how search results reflect and amplify racial hierarchy; more broadly applicable than its search-specific title suggests.

O'Neil, C. (2016). *Weapons of Math Destruction: How Big Data Increases Inequality and Threatens Democracy.* Crown Publishers. The most widely read popular treatment of algorithmic harm; accessible without sacrificing analytical substance.

Obermeyer, Z., Powers, B., Vogeli, C. and Mullainathan, S. (2019). 'Dissecting racial bias in an algorithm used to manage the health of populations.' *Science*, 366(6464), pp. 447–453. The healthcare algorithm study documented in Chapter 2 is a model of empirical research on algorithmic discrimination.

RACE, GENDER, AND STRUCTURAL BIAS

Barocas, S., Hardt, M. and Narayanan, A. (2019). *Fairness and Machine Learning.* fairmlbook.org. The most technically rigorous treatment of fairness definitions and their mathematical incompatibilities; accessible online in full.

Benjamin, R. (2019). *Race After Technology: Abolitionist Tools for the New Jim Code.* Polity Press. The 'New Jim Code' concept – technology that encodes existing racial hierarchy while presenting a racially neutral surface – is developed here with rigour and clarity.

Burt, C. (2021). 'Bias in AI: A Deep Dive.' *AI Research Journal.* Overview of technical approaches to bias detection and mitigation.

Costanza-Chock, S. (2020). *Design Justice: Community-Led Practices to Build the Worlds We Need.* MIT Press. Participatory design through the lens of social justice: the most developed account of what inclusive design actually requires.

West, S.M., Whittaker, M. and Crawford, K. (2019). *Discriminating Systems: Gender, Race, and Power in AI.* AI Now Institute. An audit of the diversity problem in AI development and its relationship to the bias problem in AI products.

CULTURAL DIVERSITY AND GLOBAL AI

Birhane, A. (2021). 'Algorithmic Injustice: A Relational Ethics Approach.' *Patterns*, 2(2). A philosophically rigorous critique of existing AI ethics frameworks from the perspective of relational ethics rooted in African intellectual tradition.

Bird, S. (2020). 'Decolonising Speech and Language Technology.' *Proceedings of the 28th International Conference on Computational Linguistics*, pp. 3504–3519. On the linguistic homogeneity of natural language processing systems and what decolonising NLP would require.

Mohamed, S., Png, M.T. and Isaac, W. (2020). 'Decolonial AI: Decolonial Theory as Sociotechnical Foresight in Artificial Intelligence.' *Philosophy & Technology*, 33(4), pp. 659–684. The paper that introduced decolonial framing to AI ethics is a starting point for thinking about the relationship between AI development and colonial knowledge structures.

Roberts, H. et al. (2021). 'The Chinese approach to artificial intelligence: an analysis of policy, ethics and regulation.' *AI & Society*, 36, pp. 59–77.

INDIGENOUS KNOWLEDGE AND DATA SOVEREIGNTY

Carroll, S.R. et al. (2020). 'The CARE Principles for Indigenous Data Governance.' *Data Science Journal*, 19(1). The CARE principles (Collective Benefit, Authority to Control, Responsibility, Ethics) provide the most developed framework for indigenous data governance.

First Nations Information Governance Centre. *Ownership, Control, Access and Possession (OCAP): The Path to First Nations Information Governance.* Ottawa: FNIGC, 2014. The Canadian framework for indigenous data governance: influential beyond Canada.

Tuhiwai Smith, L. (1999). *Decolonizing Methodologies: Research and Indigenous Peoples.* Zed Books. An intellectual foundation for understanding how research traditions encode colonial epistemology, relevant to AI research methodology as well as social science.

AI GOVERNANCE AND REGULATION

Bradford, A. (2020). *The Brussels Effect: How the European Union Rules the World.* Oxford University Press. The analytical framework for understanding how EU regulation becomes global regulation through commercial incentives rather than treaty negotiation.

Danaher, J. (2016). 'The Threat of Algocracy.' *Philosophy & Technology*, 29(3), pp. 245–268. On the democratic legitimacy of algorithmic governance.

Doshi-Velez, F. et al. (2017). 'Accountability of AI Under the Law.' Harvard CRCS Working Paper. A cross-disciplinary analysis of what existing legal frameworks can and cannot achieve in governing AI.

Hurley, M. and Adebayo, J. (2016). 'Credit Scoring in the Era of Big Data.' *Yale Journal of Law & Technology*, 18(1), pp. 148–216. On the use of non-traditional data in credit scoring and its discriminatory potential, the source for the Philippine credit context in Chapter 5.

Yeung, K. (2018). 'Algorithmic regulation: A critical interrogation.' *Regulation & Governance*, 12(4), pp. 505–523.

PARTICIPATORY DESIGN AND COMMUNITY GOVERNANCE

Arnstein, S. (1969). 'A Ladder of Citizen Participation.' *Journal of the American Institute of Planners*, 35(4), pp. 216–224. Fifty years old and still the standard reference for distinguishing genuine participation from consultation theatre.

Srinivasan, R. (2017). *Whose Global Village? Rethinking How Technology Shapes Our World.* New York University Press. A critical examination of how digital infrastructure embeds particular cultural assumptions about community, knowledge, and identity.

ON AI AND LABOUR

Dyer-Witheford, N., Mikkola Kjøsen, A. and Steinhoff, J. (2019). *Inhuman Power: Artificial Intelligence and the Future of Capitalism.* Pluto Press.

Prassl, J. (2018). *Humans as a Service: The Promise and Perils of Work in the Gig Economy.* Oxford University Press. On algorithmic management and its consequences for worker autonomy and accountability.

PULSE OXIMETRY AND MEDICAL AI

Daneshjou, R. et al. (2022). 'Disparities in dermatology AI performance on a diverse, curated clinical image set.' *Science Advances*, 8(32). The skin cancer AI accuracy disparity study.

Sjoding, M.W. et al. (2020). 'Racial Bias in Pulse Oximetry Measurement.' *New England*

Journal of Medicine, 383, pp. 2477–2478. The finding that pulse oximeters showed occult hypoxaemia nearly three times more often in Black patients than in white patients.

ABOUT THE AUTHOR

Gari Johnson has spent over four decades observing the sales methodology revolution from the inside – first as a nineteen-year-old managing a door-to-door artwork sales team in 1980s Australia, and later as a senior executive at enterprise software leaders, including IBM, Oracle, Salesforce, Zendesk, and Alteryx, across the Asia Pacific markets.

This journey from street-level hustle to C-suite strategy gave Johnson a unique perspective on how selling evolved from intuitive relationship-building to formalised business science. His early management experience with direct sales operations taught him that "every no gets you closer to yes". It revealed the power of authentic storytelling – practical foundations that later informed his analysis of sophisticated enterprise methodologies.

Johnson's executive career included front-row seats to defining moments in the evolution of sales: the CRM wars between Siebel and Salesforce, Oracle's aggressive competitive strategies, the emergence of subscription-economy customer-success approaches, and the recent integration of AI-powered conversational intelligence into enterprise sales processes. At Alteryx, he led significant revenue growth in the APJ region. At Zendesk, his team closed the region's largest-ever transaction. At Salesforce, he built the Service Cloud business into the largest cloud unit in APAC.

As both practitioner and observer, Johnson implemented dozens of sales methodologies across diverse cultural contexts, from Australia's direct business culture to Japan's consensus-building approaches to Singapore's relationship-focused markets. This international experience revealed both universal principles of effective selling and the cultural adaptations required for successful global methodology.

Johnson's writing combines rigorous research with irreverent humour, reflecting his belief that the best insights emerge when we can laugh at our professional pretensions while maintaining respect for genuine innovation. His analysis benefits from insider knowledge of how methodology companies operate and from an outsider perspective on their claims of effectiveness.

Currently based in Sydney's Northern Beaches, Johnson continues to advise technology companies on balancing structured approaches with authentic customer relationships. He serves as a Winning By Design Ambassador and Executive Member of Pavilion, contributing to the evolution of modern revenue operations and go-to-market strategy.

Johnson holds certifications in multiple sales methodologies, language qualifications in Japanese and Mandarin, and decades of experience working through both professional success and personal challenges – including financial difficulties, family tragedies, and health crises that taught him resilience extends far beyond quarterly quotas.

When not deconstructing the industrial complex's methodology, Johnson plays guitar, cooks elaborate meals, and travels extensively to understand cross-cultural business relationships. He remains partnered with "the most incredible woman" and is the father of two exceptional children, whose growing families provide ongoing education in negotiation and maintaining perspective.

ABOUT THE SERIES

The Algorithmic Mind is a three-book series examining the social consequences of artificial intelligence. The series began from a straightforward observation: AI systems are not neutral tools. They reflect the priorities, histories, and blind spots of the people who built them and the societies from which their training data was drawn.

Book 1 – The Mirror Problem: How AI Reflects Our Worst Selves traces the sources of AI bias across race, gender, language, culture, and geography, and examines the governance frameworks being developed to address it.

Book 2 – The Surveillance Mirror: How Technology Watches You examines how AI systems that learn from human data generate new data about human behaviour – and how that data is used by commercial and governmental actors to influence the choices people make.

Book 3 – The Human Interface: Keeping People at the Centre turns to the question of how AI systems can be designed and governed so that the humans they affect remain genuinely in control of consequential decisions about their own lives.

The three books can be read independently. They form a coherent argument when read in sequence: first, what AI reflects; then, what AI watches; finally, what AI shapes.